From the author.

Firstly, for all the beginners, congratulations on starting your Karate journey and welcome to the World Karate Family! For all the others, a sincere welcome to our Dojo! I also wish use this opportunity and extend a special thank you to Sensei Dion Risborg the founder of Jindokai Karate-Do, a life time ambassador to Traditional Japanese Shotokan Karate, a teacher, inspiration and a contributor for this book.

Wether you are a beginner or a bit more experienced practiser, this booklet is made just for you! It will make your Karate journey a little bit easier and make you feel right at home at the Dojo from the start. In the next few chapters we will introduce you to our common basic techniques, related vocabulary, and the Dojo etiquette. All and much more you need to start and continue your journey.

The purpose of this book is to familiarise you with the basic techniques and support your learning at the Dojo under the supervision of qualified martial art teachers with appropriate expertise and experience. Remember, safety first, yours and others. Don't attempt any of the techniques without supervision and advice from a qualified teacher as they might result in damage, cause injury, or hurt.

Sincerely yours, Marko Fagerroos

"karate-dō wa rei ni hajimari rei ni owaru koto o wasuruna"
Karate begins and ends with courtesy and respect
(Gichin Funakoshi).

INDEX

- DOJO KUN – CODE OF CONDUCT
- A BRIEF HISTORY OF KARATE
- WELCOME TO THE DOJO
- TOOLS AND TARGETS
- BELTS AND RANKINGS
- DACHI WAZA - STANCES
- ASHI WAZA - FOOT WORK
- KOSHI WAZA – HIP TECHNIQUE
- UKE WAZA – BLOCKS
- TSUKI WAZA – PUNCHES
- UCHI WAZA – STRIKES
- KERI-WAZA – KICKS
- KIHON - IDOU KIHON - MOVING BASICS
- KUMITE - SPARRING
- KATA - FORMS
- GRADING SYLLABUS (GENERIC)
- KARATE VOCABULARY
- 20 GUIDING PRINCIPALS OF KARATE-DO

DOJO KUN - 道場訓

HITOTSU: JINKAKU KANSEI NI TSUTOMURU KOTO
DEVELOP GOOD CHARACTER
Strive for the development of your character
一、人格完成に努むること

HITOTSU: MAKOTO NO MICHI O MAMORU KOTO
BE TRUTHFUL & SINCERE
Strive to develop the virtues of Truth and Sincerity
一、誠の道を守ること

HITOTSU: DORYOKU NO SEICHIN O YASHINAU KOTO
APPLY MAXIMUM EFFORT
Cultivate the spirit of perseverance
一、努力の精神を養うこと

HITOTSU: REIGI O OMONZURU KOTO
BE RESPECTFUL TO OTHERS
Honour the principles of good etiquette
一、礼儀を重んずること

HITOTSU: KEKKI NO YU O IMASHIMURU KOTO
MAINTAIN SELF-CONTROL
Guard against Reckless and Violent behaviour
一、血気の勇を戒むること

A BRIEF HISTORY OF KARATE

Modern Karate as we know it has develop and evolved for centuries. It originated from the southern tip of modern Japan called Okinawa (Old Ryukyu Kingdom) as an indigenous Ryukyuan martial art called 'Te' (Translates to Hand/ Martial Art). The art of Okinawan Te was mainly practiced and passed down by the 'Ryūkyū Samure' who were the feudal scholar-officials of Okinawan 'Yukatchu' class and charged with enforcing the law and providing military defence.

'Te' was mixed and heavily shaped by the Chinese martial arts from as early as 1300's till its modern history and up to 1900's due to the island kingdom's close cultural, political and commercial ties to China. Hence, it was locally known as 'Tode' meaning 'Chinese Hand' that was later changed to 'Kara-Te'. It's best-known 'styles' were called Shuri-te, Naha-te, and Tomari-te, respectively named after the cities they emerged from.

Bans on practising martial arts and rulings concerning bladed weaponry by the King of Ryukyu Kingdom in late 1400's and the continued ban on arms or importing arms after the Japanese samurai invasion in 1609 are said to have played important part and heavily influenced the evolution of the Karate as an unarmed martial art. Most of our modern Karate is based on the teachings that come from a lineage of Okinawan masters whom mastered and heavily crafted it's teaching methods between late 1700's to early 1900's.

In 1901 Karate was introduced in Okinawa's school system as an official form of physical exercise and a bit later, it was formally introduced in mainland Japan as 'KARATE-DO', 'the Way of Empty-Hand' instead of 'Chinese-Hand' to appease the political and cultural climate. There it adopted the use of white uniforms and the belt grading system that were both been used by the Judokas. It was officially recognised as a 'Martial Art' by the Japanese government in 1926.

A BRIEF HISTORY OF KARATE

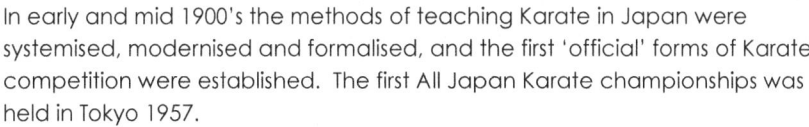

In early and mid 1900's the methods of teaching Karate in Japan were systemised, modernised and formalised, and the first 'official' forms of Karate competition were established. The first All Japan Karate championships was held in Tokyo 1957.

In today's world, as traditional Martial Art and in its modern 'Sport' forms, Karate has widely spread all around the world and is, in its all forms, the biggest Martial Art family and one of the biggest Sport families in a World with an estimated 100 million practitioners.

In the 'World Karate Family', the four styles recognised and internationally governed by the World Karate Federation are the Shotokan, Wado-ryu, Shito-ryu and Goju-ryu. That are all, amongst many others, directly connected to the ancient Okinawan 'Te', its history, traditions, and philosophy alike.

When you step through that door into your Dojo, or enter any other Dojo, respect the ways and the traditions they practise and promote. Keep your mind open, explore, discover and enjoy your journey.

Oss!

'Tora no maki'

WELCOME TO THE DOJO!

Enter the Dojo

When joining or entering a Dojo, you should expect to find a safe and family friendly professional learning place with accredited and certified teachers with appropriate expertise and experience, where all the students and teachers are at all times treated with respect and courtesy.

We recommend finding a Karate Dojo that teaches Traditional Japanese Karate, adheres to its code of conduct and values (Dojo Kun), promotes friendship, diversity, and the spirit of learning. It is also expected that students in their character and actions, in and outside of the Dojo, will positively reflect and represent those values, their Club and Karate-Do.

"karate-dō wa rei ni hajimari rei ni owaru koto o wasuruna"
Karate begins and ends with courtesy and respect
(Gichin Funakoshi).

WELCOME TO THE DOJO!

Enter the Dojo

You will Meet:

- Sensei: The main teacher
- Senpai: Other teachers and higher-grade students
- Otagai: Fellow students
- Kohai: Lower grade student

You are expected to:

- Be Punctual.
- If you arrive late, wait for permission from Sensei to join the class.
- When arriving at the training area, bow to the front to show respect.
- When arriving, greet your teacher/s (bow).
- Be respectful and courteous at all times.
- Pay attention and not to distract other students from learning.
- When pairing up, greet your training partners at the start and at the end with a bow to show respect and that we value their help in our learning.
- When teacher has given you some advice, instructed or helped you, it is courteous to bow and say 'Oss!'. 'Oss' is a specific respectful Karate expression to show that you've heard the instructions, appreciate their time, help, and advice, and to say Thank you!
- Wear a Dogi (Uniform) with an Obi (Belt).
- if you need to fix your belt or Dogi you don't do it facing Sensei or the front of the Dojo, always turn around.
- Leave your shoes outside the training area.
- Have clean and neat personal appearance.
- If applicable, have your long hair pulled back.
- Have clean and trimmed finger-and toenails (safety matter).
- Not to wear any type of jewellery, bands, or watches.
- Not to bring in or eat any food at the Dojo. (Water bottles are ok)
- After the class it is good manners to ensure the Dojo is left clean after us.

WELCOME TO THE DOJO!

In The Class

At the start, you will:
Line up (Seiretsu) according to the belt rankings.
Stand in an attention stance (Musubi Dachi)
Pay attention to the Teacher (Sensei)
Follow the class Captains lead and call, to:
- **Seiza** (Kneel down in a sitting position).
- **Mokuso** (a moment of silence and calm breathing to clear your mind).
- **Rei** (Show respect to the teachers and other students by traditional bowing). "Shomen Ni Rei, Sensei Ni Rei (Oss), Senpai Katani Rei (Oss) and Otagai Ni Rei (Oss)".

When the class is in progress, you will:
Learn from, and train with the three foundations of Karate Teaching:

KIHON: Basic techniques. Stances, footwork, blocks, punches, and kicks.
KATA: Patterns that connect techniques, stances, and movements.
KUMITE: Practise sparring/ exercise the techniques with a partner.

At the end, you will:
Line up again, exactly in a same order than in a start
Stand in the attention stance
Pay attention to the teacher
Follow the class Captains lead and call to:
- **Seiza** (Kneel).
- **Mokuso** (a moment of silence and calm breathing to clear your mind).
- **Dojo Kun** Listen and repeat after the Captain recite 'Code of Conduct'.
- **Rei** (Show respect by traditional bowing).

Stand up and thank the teachers for the class by bowing (Sensei and Senpai). This is to show respect and that we've valued their help in our learning.

道場

WELCOME TO THE DOJO!

Etiquette and formal manners

REI

TO SHOW RESPECT - FORMAL BOW

The word "Rei" is a Japanese term for showing respect and courtesy that derives from words Reiho/ Reigi that translates in showing respect, manners and etiquette, that are very important part of Japanese culture. In a Dojo we greet, thank, and show our respect to our teachers and fellow students by bowing. We bow to the front when we enter the Dojo, and during the 'Dojo Kun' to show respect to the Dojo, to our code of conduct, traditions, history and the past 'pioneers' of Karate-Do. (Shomen Ni Rei). We also greet and respond to anyone bowing to us with a bow.

Stand and bow. (Keirei, a 30 degree level bow from Musubi Dachi)

Stand upright in 'Musubi Dachi' hands down to your sides, hips and shoulders squared to front. Then, in a calm manner, bow around 30 degrees down with a straight back and keep your eyes down (As we trust and respect the person, we keep our eyes down). The Bow should be a length of one calm breath. Some martial arts like Kendo bow 15 degrees (Eshaku bow) to the opponent with the eye contact and do 30 degrees bow (Keirei) to the judges without the eye contact. Keri is also a formal business bow. Saikeirei is a utmost respect bow with 45-70 degrees.

Sit and bow (From Seiza).

From your kneeling position. Place the palm of your left hand to the floor in a front of your left knee, then repeat the same with your right hand. Bow forward with a straight back without lifting your behind off the legs, lower your forehead down and close to but, not touching the floor. Come back up in a reverse order.

REI

WELCOME TO THE DOJO!

Etiquette and formal manners

SEIZA

KNEEL – 'PROPER SITTING OR TO SIT 'CORRECTLY"

A respectful traditional Japanese sitting position where we meditate (*Mokuso), pay attention, listen, recite Dojo-Kun and bow to Shomen, Sensei, Sempai and Otagai according to the traditions.

Start by standing in Musubi Dachi. Take a small step back with your left leg and kneel down by first placing your left knee on a floor and then your right knee right next to it. (Men's knees can be two fist widths apart). Sit down on a top of your feet and place your left big toe on a top of your right big toe. Rest your hands on your thighs, (open hands, palms down). Keep an upright posture with relaxed shoulders and breath calmly.

*Mokuso', is a moment of calm breathing in silence with closed eyes that is used to clear our minds (ready for the class). After the class we can use that short moment to calm down and think about today's key points.

SEIZA

TOOLS AND TARGETS

KARA (Empty) - TE (Hand) – DO (Way)

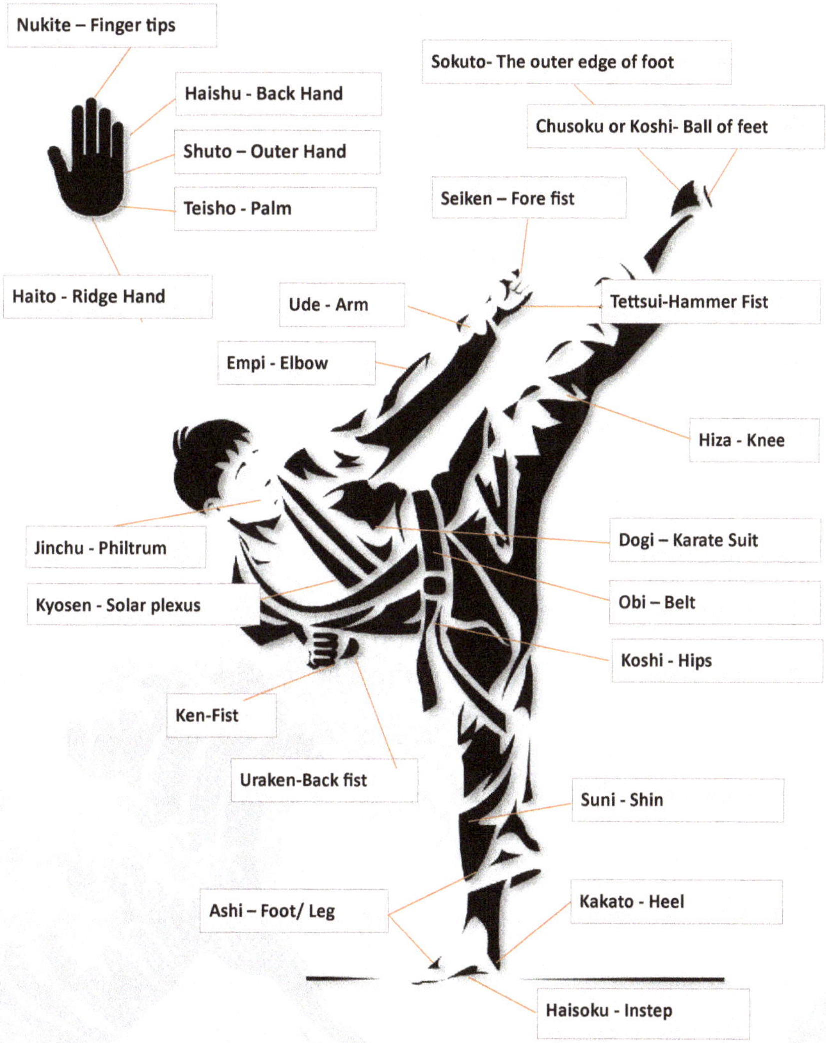

- Nukite – Finger tips
- Sokuto - The outer edge of foot
- Haishu - Back Hand
- Chusoku or Koshi - Ball of feet
- Shuto – Outer Hand
- Seiken – Fore fist
- Teisho - Palm
- Haito - Ridge Hand
- Ude - Arm
- Tettsui - Hammer Fist
- Empi - Elbow
- Hiza - Knee
- Jinchu - Philtrum
- Dogi – Karate Suit
- Kyosen - Solar plexus
- Obi – Belt
- Koshi - Hips
- Ken - Fist
- Uraken - Back fist
- Suni - Shin
- Ashi – Foot/ Leg
- Kakato - Heel
- Haisoku - Instep

BELTS AND RANKINGS

Kyu & Dan

The 'colour' belt ranks are called 'Kyu' and progress from 10th Kyu (White belt), up to the 1st Kyu (Brown belt). The Black belt levels are called Dan, and they can progress from 1st Dan upwards to 10th. Originally in Japanese Shotokan, Gichin Funakoshi had a rank system of only three colours: White 8-4th Kyu, Brown 3-1st Kyu, and Black for 1-4 Dans. Today, many different styles and clubs use their own adopted variations of the colours to suite their specific ranking systems. Ranks are earned/ achieved through skill assessment and grading tests that are based on a set skill, knowledge, and attendance criterion for each level.

Colour Belts - Kyu
10th to 1st Kyu

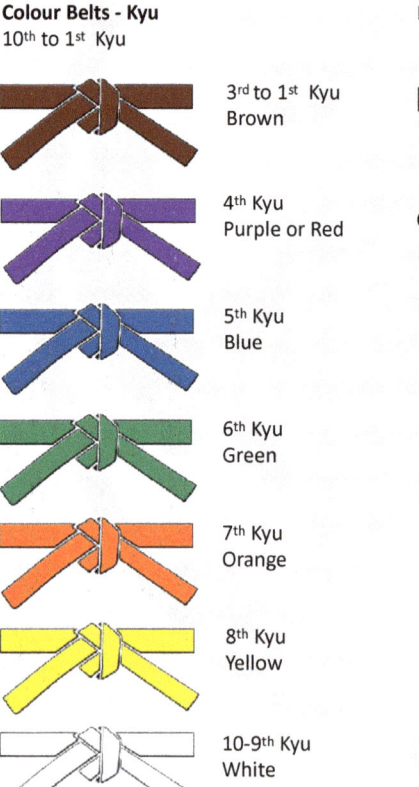

3rd to 1st Kyu
Brown

4th Kyu
Purple or Red

5th Kyu
Blue

6th Kyu
Green

7th Kyu
Orange

8th Kyu
Yellow

10-9th Kyu
White

BLACK Belts
1st to 10th Dan

Competition colours – AKA/ AO

Red represent the 'AKA' and Blue the other competitor, 'AO'.

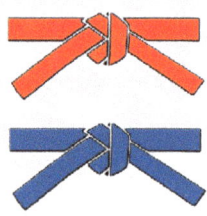

BELTS AND RANKINGS

Tying your belt (Obi)

Find the mid point of the belt and keep the manufacturers label on the left hand side. Start wrapping the belt around your waist from front to back. Cross the belt at the back and bring both ends to the front. Cross the left over right, then tug it under and upwards. Tighten and fold over. Now tie the other side around it and tighten the knot. Both ends should be equal length and the manufacturers label should end up on the same side than the Gi label (RH)

1. Find the mid point of the belt. Start wrapping around your waist from the front.

2. Cross at the back and bring both ends to the front.

3. Keep tight, cross left (A) over right (B)

4. Tug (A) under both and pull up. Tighten.

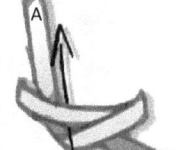

5. Fold (A) over.

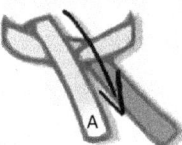

6. Bring (B) across and under (A).

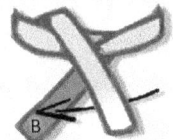

7. Bring (B) up and start folding it around (A)

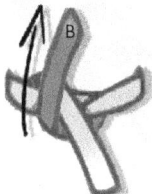

8. Tie (B) around the (A) and tighten. The badge of your belt should end up on a same side with the badge on your dogi

# DACHI WAZA - STANCES

Stances 'Dachi' are the first step in learning Karate. With the stances, we root our feet to the ground for balance, strength and stability. They are designed to developed, increase and maximise our striking power, acceleration and speed that are all generated from ground up through our stances and footwork. To be able to successfully perform and deliver all the other techniques, you will first need to learn and master the stances together with the correct footwork. The good news is, it's all based in physics and sport science, so no magic tricks or invisible forces are required, just following instructions, hard work, repetition, repetition, repetition and persistence. Stances also play important part in the manners, formalities and correct etiquette in Karate-do.

To successfully shift a threatening situation into our advantage or effectively deliver a decisive technique greatly depend on our abilities to use and manipulate the stances and footwork.

DACHI WAZA - STANCES

SHIZENTAI 'NATURAL STANCES'

MUSUBI DACHI
FORMAL ATTENTION STANCE

Used for formal bowing (Rei) and when lining up and paying attention to the teacher at the start and at the end of the class. Hands on sides, upright posture, hips and shoulders squared to the front. Heels together, toes apart in 45 degree angle. Weight 50/50 on both legs.

HEISOKU DACHI
FEET TOGETHER STANCE

An upright, 'transitional'/ 'ready' stance. Used in several katas. Upright posture, hips and shoulders squared to the front. Feet together. Weight 50/50 on both legs.

HEISOKU DACHI

MUSUBI DACHI

DACHI WAZA - STANCES

SHIZENTAI 'NATURAL STANCES'

HEIKO DACHI
PARALLEL STANCE, FEET STRAIGHT

Ready' stance (Yoi). Used when listening instructions or waiting for a go/ start (Hajime) command. A shoulder width upright stance. Hips and shoulders squared to the front and toes pointing straight forward. Weight 50/50 on both legs.

HACHIJI DACHI
PARALLEL STANCE FEET OPEN

As above with feet open at 45° angle. Also used as a 'Ready' stance (Yoi) in Kihon, Kata and Kumite or for paying attention. Weight 50/50 on both legs.

HEIKO DACHI

HACHIJI DACHI

# DACHI WAZA - STANCES

ZENKUTSU DACHI
FRONT STANCE

Our most common stance in training. Both feet are pointing forward with your back-foot slightly angled outwards at 15°. Stance should be a shoulder width wide and twice as long.

Keep both heels firmly anchored to the ground and your back leg fully extended. You should feel your back leg (from heel up) as a driving force pushing your hips forward. Keep the front knee aligned and bent directly over the front foot. 60-70% of your weight should be on a front leg. Keep an upright posture with your shoulders and hips parallel to the floor. Hips and shoulders can be squared to the front (Shomen), open at 45° (Hanmi), or rotated into reversed position (Gyaku-Hanmi).

SHOMEN
HIPS FORWARD

HANMI
HIPS 'OPEN' AT 45°

ZENKUTSU DACHI

DACHI WAZA - STANCES

KOKUTSU DACHI
BACK STANCE (KO-BACK, KUTSU-BENT)

This stance is mainly used for defensive techniques or combinations. Stand with both of your heels on a same line, two shoulder widths apart. Your front foot and the front knee are aligned and pointing straight forward. The back-foot and its knee are aligned and pointing directly to the side at 90° angle, or just slightly backwards. Keep both heels firmly anchored to the ground, sit firmly on your bent back leg and push both knees slightly outwards.

Your hips and shoulders are open to the side at 45° angle (Hanmi). 70% of your weight should be sitting firmly on your bent back leg. The back knee should be aligned with, and directly over the back foot. Keep your front leg slightly bent and do not 'lock' the front knee. Keep an upright posture with your shoulders and hips parallel to the floor.

HANMI
HIPS 'OPEN' AT 45°

KOKUTSU DACHI

DACHI WAZA - STANCES

KIBA DACHI
HORSE RIDING STANCE

This stance is mainly for sideways movement and techniques aimed to the side. Hips are squared to the front, feet are parallel two shoulder widths apart, toes pointing forward. Keep both heels firmly anchored to the ground and keep pushing your knees outwards. Sit/ squat down with your weight directly above your heels, 50/50 on both legs. Knee angle should be the same than in a front stance. Keep an upright posture with a straight back. Shoulders and hips parallel to the floor.

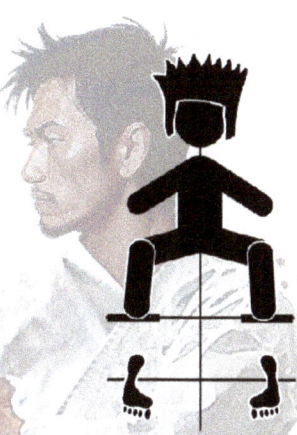

KIBA DACHI

SHIKO DACHI
Similar to Kiba Dachi, but your feet are open to 45° angle with toes pointing outwards. (Knees aligned with the feet).

KIBA DACHI

 # DACHI WAZA - STANCES

KOSA DACHI
CROSS STANCE

Often used as transitional move between stances and changes in direction. Generally, in defence, the hips are open in 'Hanmi' and in offence the hips are squared to the front in 'Shomen'. The front foot is rooted flat to the ground with its toes pointing forward. Keep the front knee aligned and bent directly over the front foot. The back foot is 'stepped' in and brought around to the outside of the front foot with its toes pointing towards the outsole of the front foot. Only the ball of the back foot is on the ground.

The shin and the knee of the back foot are firmly pressed against the back of the front leg for strength and stability. Weight sitting 70-80% on a front foot. Keep an upright posture with your shoulders and hips parallel to the floor.

KOSA DACHI

 # DACHI WAZA - STANCES

NEKO ASHI DACHI

CAT STANCE

In this stance, first square your shoulders and hips to the front and open your back foot outwards to 30-degree angle. Then sit your weight straight down on your bent back leg. Sit with a straight back, over and just slightly behind the ankle of your back foot. Next, slide the other foot forward (one foot length apart) and rest it there, heel up on the ball of the foot.

Both legs are bent, the back leg is bent at 45-degree angle with 80-90% of your weight sitting on it. Your back knee should be aligned with your back foot. Your front foot and front knee are aligned and pointing forward, the front foot is resting gently on its toes or on the ball of the foot.

NEKO ASHI DACHI

DACHI WAZA - STANCES

RENOJI DACHI
L-SHAPE STANCE

Another upright, more 'natural' stance. Often used as transitional stance between' kata techniques and directions. Hips are open to Hanmi. Stand with both heels on a same line, one foot apart. Toes of your front foot should point straight forward and back foot to your side in a 90° angle. Keep both heels firmly anchored to the ground. Weight 60% on your back leg. Keep an upright posture, shoulders and hips parallel to the floor. (This stance, if you pull your back foot slightly in to form a 'T-shape with your feet, is called '**TEIJI DACHI**').

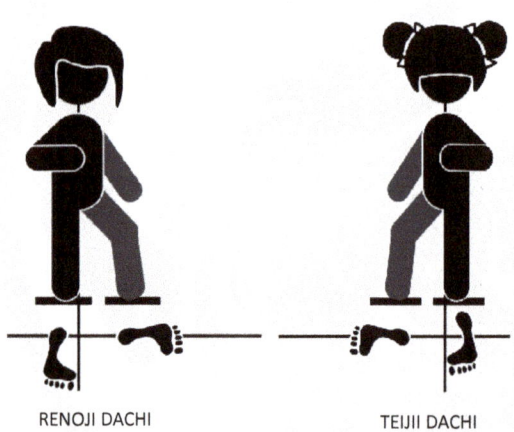

RENOJI DACHI   TEIJII DACHI

Worth of further research: Kamae Dachi, Hizakutsu Dachi, Ashi Dachi, Tsuru-Ashi-Dachi, Sagi-Ashi-Dachi, Fudo-Dachi, Sanchin Dachi and postures like Ryoken Koshi Kamae (Two fists on a hip posture).

DACHI WAZA - STANCES

LEARNING PLAN

MUSUBI DACHI

NEKO ASHI DACHI

HEISOKU DACHI

HEIKO DACHI

ZENKUTSU DACHI

KOKUTSU DACHI

KIBA DACHI

KOSA DACHI

RENOJI DACHI

腰 KOSHI WAZA - HIPS

Hip movement, hip rotation, and their correct alignment are essential to speed and power generation. Learn to control and drive all your moves with the hips and feel the connection from 'heel up' to your hips. Practise using your hips and abdomen with your blocks, punches, kicks, steps and turns by pushing and turning your body 'from' the hips and driving all the moves from your 'core'. With practise, you will learn to support and strengthen your, moves, blocks, kicks and punches with your hips and core.

Don't underestimate the importance of using and 'conditioning' your hips.

Generally, in offence the hips are squared up to the front in Shomen, and in defence open to your side at 45 degree angle in Hanmi. The position where our hips are rotated to the opposite side is called 'Gyaku-Hanmi', that is a 'reversed hip' position (Try this with a reverse side Uchi-Uke).

SHOMEN
HIPS FORWARD

HANMI
HIPS 'OPEN' AT 45°

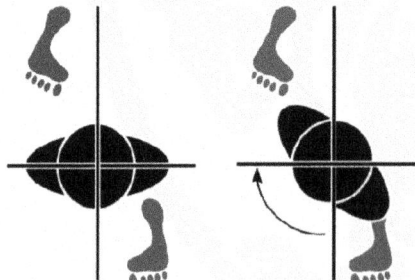

Practise the hip rotation and condition your hips by standing in a Zenkutsu Dachi and alternate the hips from Shomen to Hanmi.

You can do this together with any block and punch combination. Assist the move and the rotation with a proper Hikite (Retuning hand).

Keep upright, don't lean, and keep your hips and shoulders parallel to the floor. Keep your front knee stationary, bent over and aligned with your foot. Keep both feet firmly rooted to the floor.

ASHI SABAKI - FOOTWORK

Ashi means foot, and Sabaki means movement.

When it comes to self defence, using your feet (Walk or run) to distance yourself from a dangerous situation and getting out of the harm's way is probably the most effective technique among situational awareness there is.

In a competition or fight situation, the fighter with better footwork will most likely have the control and the advantage over the other. Having good footwork means having the ability and knowledge to place your feet exactly how, when and where they need to be.

Footwork:

AYUMI ASHI - Normal heel to toe walking, step through

SURI ASHI - As in Ayumi Ashi, but with sliding feet

TSUGI ASHI - Shuffle step, slide the back foot in and then advance with the front foot. Back leg doesn't pass your front leg. No body rotation.

YORI ASHI - Shuffle step, step the front foot out, then slide along your back foot.

CHIDORI ASHI - Step across sideways, one foot in front of the other. style of walking on the edge of the feet.

SURIKOMI ASHI - Sliding step across sideways without rotating your body.

MAWATTE - Turn around

TAI SABAKI - Shifting body position out from the line of attack.

 ASHI SABAKI - FOOTWORK

Ashi means foot, and Sabaki means movement.

Moving in a Front Stance.

Start by pushing your front knee and hips forward. 1. Bring your back foot in, square your hips, and transfer your entire weight to your front foot. Keep its heel anchored to the ground.

Keep sliding the back foot straight forward and past the front foot. Maintain your height and upright posture with your hips and shoulders parallel to the floor and remember, 'momentum here is straight forward not up or down'. Then use your leg with the weight on it to push your hips and core strongly forward (push from heel up), transfer your weight and extend to a full Zenkutsu Dachi.

ASHI SABAKI - FOOTWORK

Ashi means foot, and Sabaki means movement.

Moving in a Front Stance.

When moving backwards, bring your front foot back in, square your hips and transfer your weight on the back leg. Keep the momentum going, push backwards and extend to full Zenkutsu Dachi

ASHI SABAKI - FOOTWORK

Moving in a Back Stance.

To start, push your front knee and hips forward, bring your back foot in, square your hips, and transfer your entire weight to your front foot. Keep its heel anchored to the ground.

Keep sliding the back foot straight forward and past the front foot. Keep the weight on a same leg, maintain your height, keep an upright posture, hips and shoulders parallel to the floor and remember, 'momentum here is straight forward not up or down'. Without stopping, use the gained momentum and speed with your rotating hips (opening to Hanmi), to extend in full Kokutsu Dachi. (Rotate your hips open 'on and around' the back heel).

 ASHI SABAKI - FOOTWORK

Moving in a Back Stance.

When moving backwards, maintain your height, keep the knees bent and an upright posture. Bring your front foot back in, square your hips and keep the weight on a same leg. Keep the momentum going, push backwards, open your hips, transfer your weight and extend to full Kokutsu Dachi

足 ASHI SABAKI - FOOTWORK

Moving sideways/ in Horse-Riding Stance.

Moving sideways. Maintain your upright upper body posture and your head height. Keep your squared shoulders and hips parallel to the floor. To start, without rotating your hips or shoulders, bring in, slide, or step your foot across, past, and right next to the other foot. Transfer your entire weight on it and keep its heel anchored to the ground. Then slide or step the other foot out to your side, extend, and transfer your weight to full Kiba Dachi.

SURIKOMI ASHI

Step or slide your foot across the other one without turning your hips.

SIDEWAYS STEP

足 ASHI SABAKI - FOOTWORK

Suri Ashi - Sliding steps:

YORI ASHI

Expand and Contract. Move, in any direction by first pushing/ sliding your leading foot out (Expanding to a longer stance), then dragging the other foot in but, not past the leading foot (Contracting back to normal size stance).

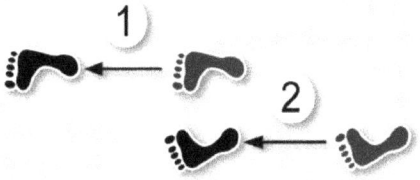

TSUGI ASHI

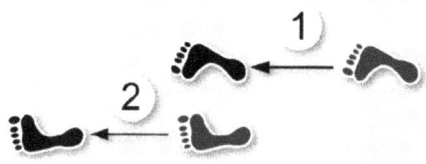

"Contract and Expand. Move in any direction by first pulling/ sliding your foot in (To a smaller stance) but, not past the other foot. Then pushing/ sliding the other foot out and 'expanding' back to a 'normal' size stance.

AYUMI ASHI.

Step your foot past the other. Sequence as in normal walking. In any Direction

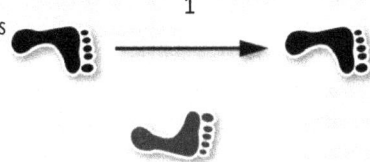

 ASHI SABAKI - FOOTWORK

TURNING

MAWATTE, (Inside Turn, on a front heel)

180 Degree Turn. TURN AROUND ON A SPOT - SHORT INSIDE TURN (CHANGES LEADING FOOT)

In this turn we lead the turn with our back foot and pivot around the front heel. Maintain your 'upright' upper body posture and your head height with shoulders and hips parallel to the floor. Keep your elbows in and your centre of gravity low.

From Zenkutsu Dachi. Start moving your back foot across your back (1), keep your weight on the front heel and pivot 180° around it to face the opposite direction (2). Then, without stopping, push your hips and foot forward to extend in a full Zenkutsu Dachi.

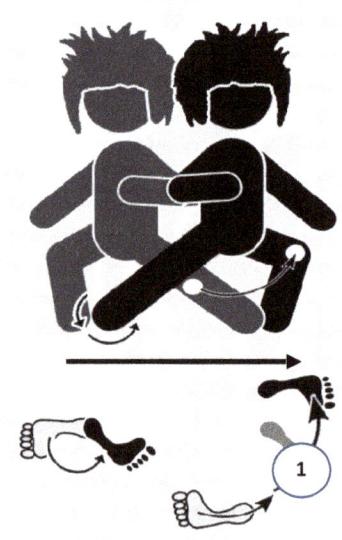

INSIDE TURN – TURN AROUND

ASHI SABAKI - FOOTWORK

TURNING

MAWATTE, (Inside Turn, on a front heel)

180 Degree Turn. TURN AROUND ON A SPOT - SHORT INSIDE TURN (CHANGES THE LEADING FOOT)

ASHI SABAKI - FOOTWORK

TURNING

D-TURN, (Outside turn, on a back heel)

TURN AROUND – LONG OUTSIDE TURN (LANDS ON THE SAME LEADING FOOT)

In this turn, we lead with the front foot. In one continuous motion, start sliding your front foot (in a straight line) backwards and transfer (sit) your entire weight on your back foot. Without stopping, use the gained speed, momentum, and your hips to pivot around the back heel as close as you can to the opposite direction. Keep upright, weight on your back foot/ heel and your centre of gravity low. Then push your your hips and foot forward to fully extend to Zenkutsu Dachi. (Keep the back heel anchored to the ground).

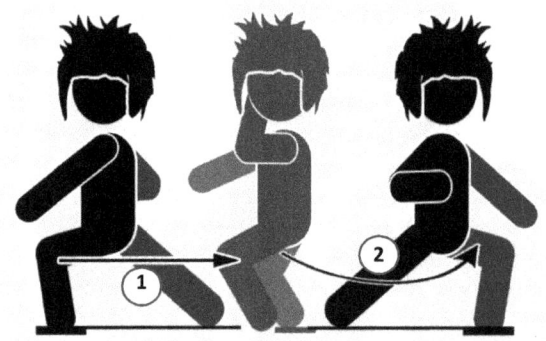

D – TURN, 180 DEGREES
The 'D' in D-Turn represents the shape of the path your front foot follows.

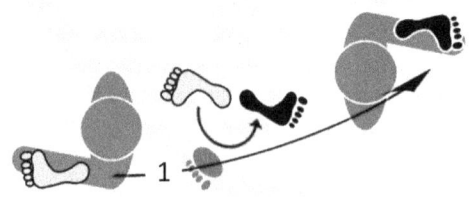

ASHI SABAKI - FOOTWORK

TURNING

D-TURN, (Outside turn, on a back heel)
TURN AROUND – LONG OUTSIDE TURN (LANDS ON THE SAME LEADING FOOT)

Practice these turns from full Zenkutsu-Dachi with Gedan-Barai through the centre of your gravity to another Zenkutsu-Dachi with a Gedan-Barai. Remember to keep upright, elbows in, and your weight low and centred during these turns.

ASHI SABAKI - FOOTWORK

TURNING

90 Degree turn, to the side.

To the right (Migi) from a right-hand stance, or to the left (Hidari) from a left-hand stance. Leading with a front foot, weight on a back heel and driving with the hips. Shifts your direction of travel directly to your side. Start by transferring your weight on the back heel then turn and step/ slide the front foot directly to your side and extend into full front stance by pushing strongly from the heel and extending to full stance.

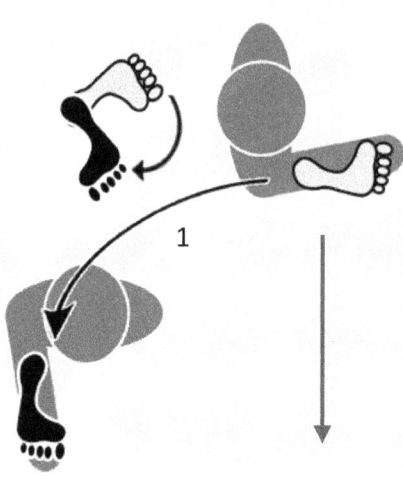

ASHI SABAKI - FOOTWORK

TURNING

90 Degree turn, to the side.

(LANDS ON THE SAME LEADING FOOT)

Pull the front foot slightly back, transfer your weight to the back heel, turn and extend to full stance.

90 DEGREE TURN ON AND AROUND THE BACK HEEL

ASHI SABAKI - FOOTWORK

TURNING

270 Degree turn, Around the back foot

In this ¾ turn, we lead with the back foot. In one continuous motion, from Zenkutsu Dachi, keep the weight on the front foot and start moving your back foot across your back. Use your body and hips to pivot around the front heel. Without stopping, use the gained speed, momentum, and your hips to continue turning as close to 270° as you can. Keep your elbows in and the centre of your gravity low. Then push forward (from heel up) and fully extend to Zenkutsu Dachi. (Keep your heel anchored to the ground). Practise this turn until you can do it in one fluid motion without losing your balance.

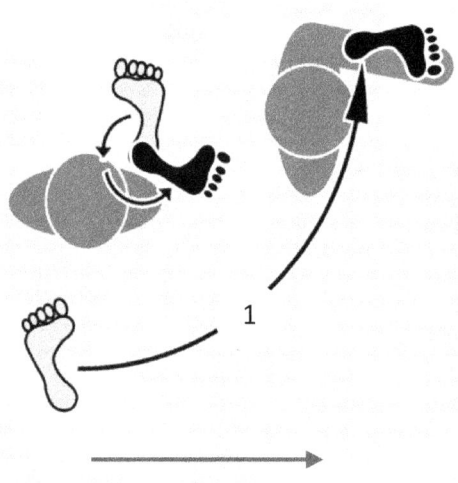

AROUND THE BACK FOOT TURN

ASHI SABAKI - FOOTWORK

TURNING

270 Degree turn, Around the back foot

Keep the weight on the front foot, slide the back foot across your back and pivot around on the front heel. Keep your weight low and centred.

270 DEGREE TURN

 ASHI SABAKI - FOOTWORK
LEARNING PLAN

MOVING IN A FRONT STANCE	180° MAWATTE (INSIDE)
MOVING IN A BACK STANCE	180° D-TURN (OUTSIDE)
MOVING IN A RIDING STANCE	270° AROUND THE BACK
AYUMI ASHI	TAI SABAKI (SHIFT OUT FROM THE LINE OF ATTACK)
YORI ASHI	
TSUGI ASHI	
SURIKOMI ASHI	
90° RIGHT & LEFT TURN	

UKE WAZA - BLOCKS

Uke derives from a Japanese word 'Ukeru' to receive. In Karate we can use our 'blocking' techniques to our advantage in multiple ways in order to protect ourselves from harm. In basic level we mostly use the 'Uke' techniques with the wrist and forearm action and the circular sweeping techniques (Gedan Barai) to receive attacks.

Commonly in defence, to 'receive', that is to deflect, divert or catch a punch or a kick, and to change our position from disadvantage to advantage one. We also use those same techniques to clear path, catch, grapple, break or strike, and as precursors to our counter strikes in short combination techniques (Renzoku-Waza).

As with the other techniques, to be effective, you must learn to use them together with your hips, (Koshi-Waza), stance techniques (Dachi-Waza) and footwork (Ashi-Waza).

SOTO-UKE

UKE WAZA - BLOCKS

GEDAN BARAI
Lower (Sweep) Block

A lower 'sweeping' block. To defend against lower level attacks (Gedan level). Unlike 'Uke-Blocks, Gedan Barai is a circular sweep, and does not have the turning wrist action.

Bring your fist up to your ear with its palm facing the ear. Ensure your elbow has travelled across and past the centreline of your chest. Now, point your other fist with (straight) arm to the 'target'. From here, together with the Hikite, and your hips opening to Hanmi, leading with the back of the fist, sweep the fist down along the pointed arm, and in a circular motion, fully extend it above your front knee.

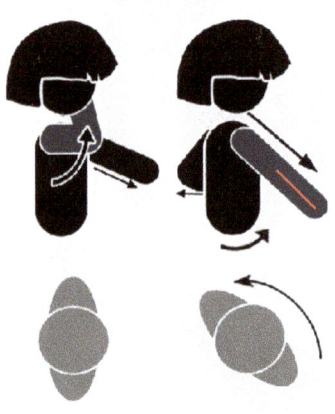

GEDAN-BARAI

UKE WAZA - BLOCKS

GEDAN BARAI

Lower (Sweep) Block

Fist should end up knuckles up, directly above the front knee and aligned with the knee and the shoulder. Ensure your fist is clenched tight to avoid any injury if it's hit or kicked on during practise.

GEDAN-BARAI

# UKE WAZA - BLOCKS

AGE-UKE

'RISING' OR 'UPPER' BLOCK.

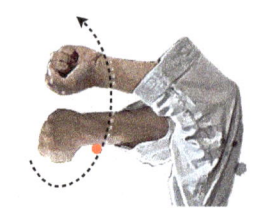
Wrist rotation

To defend against higher level attacks aimed at the head (Jodan level). Start with the fist on your side (from Hikite position). Brush it straight up across the centre-front of your chest with its palm facing in. Once your fist reaches the Jodan level (just under the chin), bring the fist and the upper-arm up across your face in a 45 degree angle, and level them, with the elbow, slightly above and in a front of your forehead (Hitae). Elbow should end up aligned with the shoulder. (At the next level, once blocked, open your blocking hand and capture the opponent's arm. Tsukami-Uke). Leave a sufficient gap between the forearm and your forehead and don't block your view to the front or to the side with your arm.

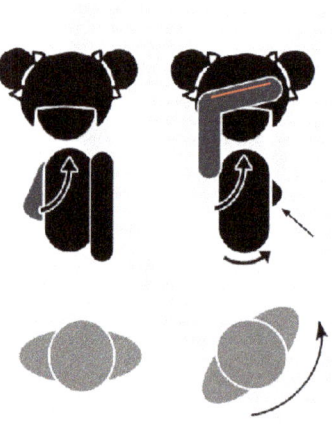

AGE-UKE

UKE WAZA - BLOCKS

AGE-UKE

'RISING' OR 'UPPER' BLOCK.

'Receive' the attack with (.) the back of your forearm or wrist while in upwards motion and deflect it by rotating your wrist and forearm around (Inner-upper-arm to front).

UKE WAZA - BLOCKS

SOTO-UKE

FROM OUTSIDE TO IN BLOCK

From 'outside-in' block. Like the Uchi-Uke, mainly used to protect your body from attacks at the 'Chudan' level. Start, with your hips and shoulders squared to the front. Bring your clenched fist up to your side with its palm and inner arm facing outwards, elbow at the shoulder level in a 90-degree angle. At the same time, straighten your other arm in a front of you and point it to the target at the Chudan level.

Then, together with the 'Hikite', in a circular motion, use your hips and shoulders to bring the bent arm (palm first), directly in a front you and rotate/ flick the wrist around to bring the back of your fist to the front. Fist should end up aligned with the shoulder, at the shoulder height, elbow pointing down and bent at 90 degrees. Receive the attack with your inner wrist or inner arm and deflect it by rotating/ flipping the wrist and forearm around. Receive and deflect, do not hit.

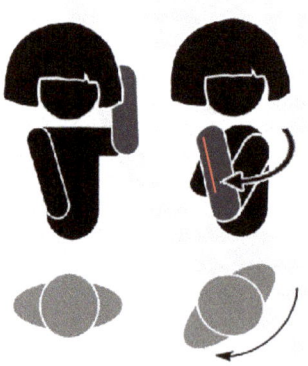

SOTO-UKE

 # UKE WAZA - BLOCKS

SOTO-UKE

FROM OUTSIDE TO IN BLOCK

Receive the attack with (•) the flat inner wrist or with inside of your forearm (not the side bone) and deflect it with a wrist action by rotating/ flipping the wrist and forearm around. Receive and deflect, do not hit

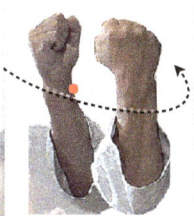

Wrist rotation

SOTO UKE

UKE WAZA - BLOCKS

UCHI-UKE
FROM INSIDE TO OUT BLOCK

From 'inside - out' motion block. Mainly used to protect your body from attacks at the 'Chudan' level. To start, stand with your hips squared to the front (in 'Shomen'), straighten your other arm and point it to the 'target' at the Chudan level. Then, bring the fist of your blocking arm across your chest, under, and all the way to the other side of the straightened arm at the shoulder height with the back of the fist pointing in.

Then, simultaneously with the Hikite and hip rotation (to 'Hanmi'), bring the bent arm directly in a front you and rotate the back of your fist to the front. Elbow should still be pointing down, aligned with the shoulder, and bent at 90 degrees. Your blocking fist should be at the shoulder level, knuckles to the front.

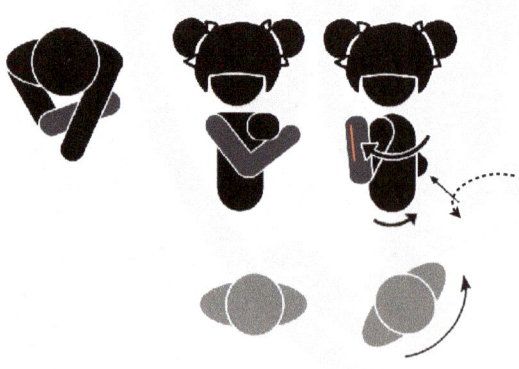

UCHI UKE

UKE WAZA - BLOCKS

UCHI-UKE
FROM INSIDE TO OUTSIDE BLOCK

Receive the attack with (•) the flat outer wrist or with back of your forearm (not the side bone) and deflect it with a wrist action by rotating/ flipping the wrist and forearm around. Receive and deflect, do not hit

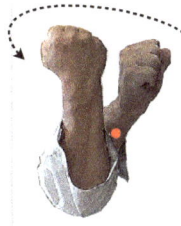

Wrist rotation

UCHI UKE

UKE WAZA - BLOCKS

SHUTO-UKE
KNIFE HAND BLOCK

Bring your (open) right hand up to your left ear with the palm facing the ear. (Brush it up across your chest). Ensure your elbow has travelled past the centreline of your chest. At the same time, straighten your left arm in a front of you and point it to the target at Chudan level.

From here, leading with the thumb side (Haito) sweep the back of your right hand down along the top of your left arm. Once your right hand reaches the left elbow, together with the left hand 'Hikite' and rotating your hips open to Hanmi, sweep your hand to the right side (In a front of your shoulder) and rotate/ snap the hand around its wrist to 'Shuto'.

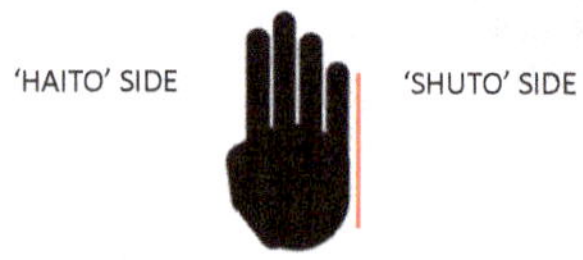

'HAITO' SIDE   'SHUTO' SIDE

SHUTO UKE

UKE WAZA - BLOCKS

SHUTO-UKE / SHUTO UCHI
KNIFE HAND BLOCK/ STRIKE

Your elbow and hand should end up aligned and in a front of your shoulder with the fingertips at shoulder level, elbow pointing down and bent around 90 degrees. Receive the attack with (•) the thumb-side or the back-hand side of the wrist and deflect it by rotating/ snapping the wrist and hand around to Shuto.

Wrist rotation

SHUTO UKE

UKE WAZA - BLOCKS

MOROTE UKE
AUGMENTED/ SUPPORTED BLOCK

A very versatile supported block. Similar to Uchi-Uke but supported by the back arm for strength and power. Used in all stances and in both, defence and offence. Moving forward its often used to 'over power' the opponent and in 'block and strike' combibations where the supporting hand strikes immediately after the block or after 'off balancing' the opponent.

UKE WAZA - BLOCKS

LEARNING PLAN

GEDAN BARAI	OSAE UKE
AGE UKE	MANJI UKE
SOTO UKE	
UCHI UKE	
SHUTO UKE	
MOROTE UKE	
JUJI UKE	
KAKIWAKE UKE	

TSUKI WAZA - PUNCHES

Punches, the 'Zuki' are delivered in a straightforward (Thrusting) motion with the two knuckles of your index and middle finger ('Seiken)' of your tightly clenched fist (Ken). It is important to understand from the start that we control the reach of our punches with our stances and footwork, not by overextending our arms or by leaning our body. You should also keep in mind that the main contributor for your striking power is your speed and your technique, not your strength.

'KEN, SEIKEN, HIKITE & ZUKI

FIST, KNUCKLES, A RETURNING HAND TECHNIQUE AND PUNCH

Correct karate punch start with a correctly formed fist (Ken), is launched with a correct hip movement, delivered with correct arm extension technique, supported with the 'returning hand 'hikite' technique and completed by connecting the 'Seiken' to the target with correct timing, maximum acceleration, speed and accuracy to the maximum impact.

KEN/ SEIKEN

FORM A FIST

Fully extend both of your arms with open hands directly in a front of your chest at the Chudan level (Just below your shoulder level, in a front of your solar plexus) with palms facing down (Thumbs in). Then, without moving your hands, wrists, or arms, roll your fingers in to form a fist, and seal them with the thumbs on a top of the fingers. Ensure the top of the wrist and the fist are levelled straight like a ruler and the 'Seiken', (The two knuckles of the index and middle finger) are pointing directly to the 'target'. Keep the fists together side by side.

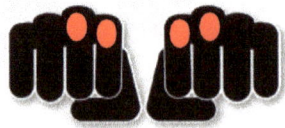

'Seiken' are the two knuckles of the index and middle finger.

TSUKI WAZA - PUNCHES

FIST TURN AND 'HIKITE
RETURNING HAND TECHNIQUE

With both of your straight arms and clenched fists still directly in a front of your chest, without changing their height or alignment, start the 'Hikite' (Returning Hand Technique) by rolling your fist out and over until the back of the fist is facing down. From here, pull the fist (with your elbow) straight backwards. Keep your elbow in and ensure your arm is brushing against the side of your body, pull it back until your clenched fist is on your side with the back of it facing downwards and knuckles facing the target. Keep your elbow tucked in. In this position, when your hips are squared back to the front, your fist should have a direct line to the target.

HIKITE, 'RETURNING HAND'
Imagine using your elbow to hit a target directly behind your back. 'Hikite' should be as fast and 'snappy' as the punch or the block performed with it.

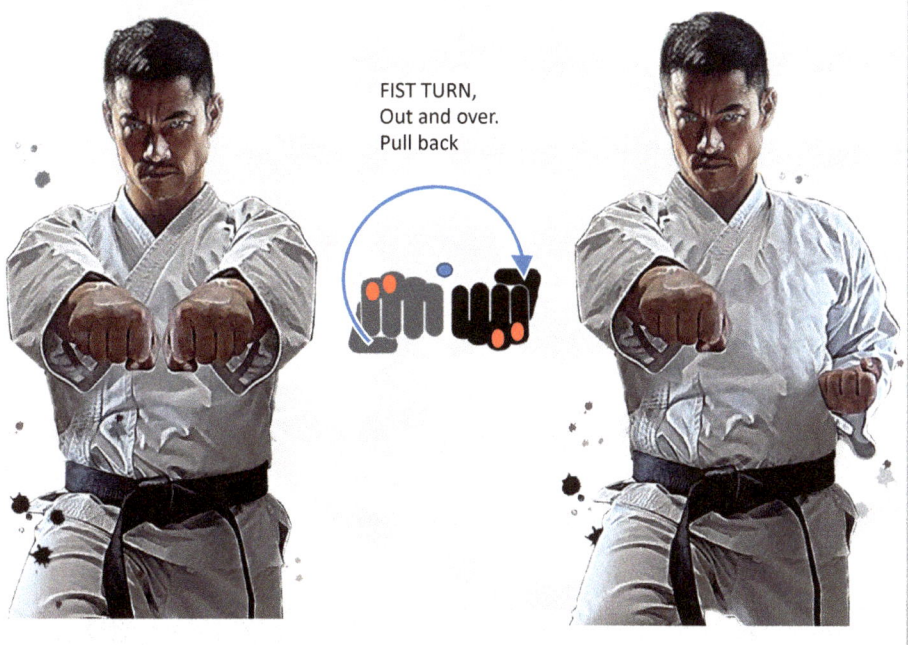

FIST TURN,
Out and over.
Pull back

突き TSUKI WAZA - PUNCHES

LEARNING ZUKI/ TSUKI
THE PUNCH

After performing the 'Hikite', keep your fist (Knuckles down) on a hip and turn your hips to hanmi.

Launch the punch from, and with the hips rotating from 'Hanmi' to 'Shomen' (Hips squared to front). Aim and move your fist in a straight line towards the target. Ensure the side of your arm keeps brushing along your side, keep the elbow in and your knuckles down until your elbow leaves the side of your body. Then in one 'snapping' motion, fully extend your arm and roll your fist back in (Knuckles up) and deliver the punch with the 'Seiken'. In this exercise, your fist should end up back in our starting position where the fists and arms were side by side, thumbs together.

SHOMEN
HIPS FORWARD

HANMI
HIPS 'OPEN' AT 45°

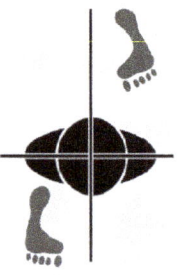

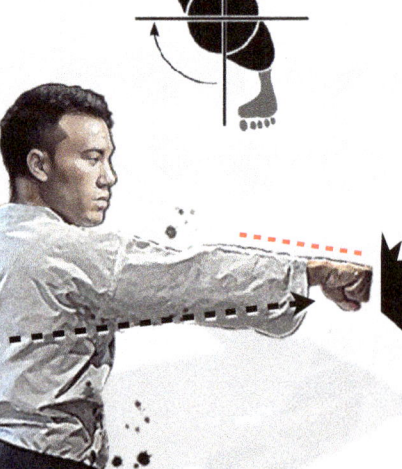

*Top of the forearm, wrist and the back of the fist must be aligned straight. An impact on a fist with bent wrist will likely lead to an injury.

突き TSUKI WAZA - PUNCHES

LEARNING ZUKI/ TSUKI
THE PUNCH

When punching, keep upright, shoulders squared to front. Don't lean forward or overextend your arm. Keep the punch straight, elbow in and don't allow your elbow or fist to 'circle out'. Control your striking distance with your stance and footwork, not by leaning forward or overextending the arm or shoulder.

JODAN LEVEL

CHUDAN LEVEL

- Tightly clenched fists
- Straight firm wrist
- Launch with hip rotation
- Strong Hikite
- Strong core
- Keep both elbows in
- Upright Posture
- Don't lean forward

Practise by repeating both the Hikite and Zuki simultaneously with opposite hands. Once you're comfortable with this technique, practise it with the emphasis on correct hip rotation (Koshi Waza) and 'Hikite' to launch, speed up and power up the punch.

突き TSUKI WAZA - PUNCHES

CHOKU ZUKI
FRONT PUNCH

Choku Zuki, a straightforward punch on the leading foot side with the hips and shoulders squared to the front (Shomen). Delivered with 'Seiken'.

SHOMEN
HIPS AND SHOULDERS FORWARD

突き TSUKI WAZA - PUNCHES

OI-ZUKI
THROUGH STEP PUNCH.

In '**Oi-Zuki**', the punch is delivered with the through step on the leading foot side. Its launched from the hips and connected to the target exactly the same time with the landing of the foot. It combines the power and speed of the punch, the forward thrusted hips and the 'through step'.

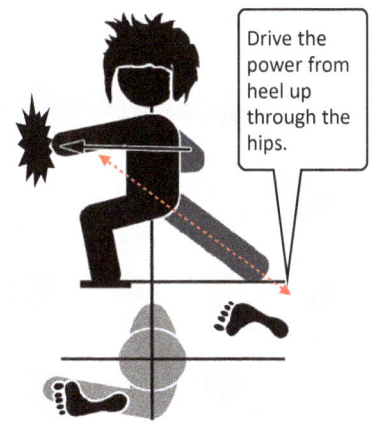

Drive the power from heel up through the hips.

'OI ZUKI'/ LUNGE PUNCH

突き TSUKI WAZA - PUNCHES

OI-ZUKI
THROUGH STEP PUNCH.

Keep upright, don't lean forward or overextend your arm. Keep the punch straight, elbow in and don't allow your elbow or fist to 'circle out'. Control your striking distance with your stance and the footwork, not by leaning forward or overextending the arm or shoulder. The striking power is a combination of your strength, speed and momentum, that are generated from the ground up through the strength of your back leg, forward thrusted and rotating hips, core muscles, shoulders and extending arm all the way to the fist delivered with correct techniques and timing.

Punch should connect to the target exactly the same time with the landing of the foot

突き TSUKI WAZA - PUNCHES

GYAKU ZUKI
REVERSE PUNCH

A straightforward punch with the 'Seiken' like Choku-Zuki but, delivered on the 'reverse side' (back foot side). The 'Reverse' Punch is launched from, and with the hips rotating from 'Hanmi' to 'Shomen' after 'landing' the front foot (if stepping through). Often as a part of fast and short combinations (Renzoku Waza) following another technique like Kizame, Jodan Oi-zuki, or a Uke-Waza, taking full advantage of the power and speed of extending back leg and the hip rotation. (Power from heel up through the hips).

Punch is launched from, and with the hips rotating from 'Hanmi' to 'Shomen' after 'landing' the front foot (if stepping through).

突き TSUKI WAZA - PUNCHES

KIZAME ZUKI
'LEADING' PUNCH

Kizame-Zuki is a quick, fast, and powerful punch with 'extra reach. It's a straightforward punch delivered from the leading foot side with 'Seiken' like Choku-Zuki or Oi-Zuki but delivered with the hips and shoulders rotated open to 'Hanmi' for extended reach. Usually delivered with extending forward step like in Yori-Ashi, or with a 'step through' step as in Oi-Zuki.

KIZAME ZUKI

HANMI
HIPS 'OPEN' AT 45°

打 UCHI WAZA - STRIKES

Punched are delivered with Seiken (Front knuckless) and the Strikes using any other parts of the fist, hand and arm. Like the back and sides of the hand and fist including palms, fingers and elbows. Strikes are usually delivered in a circular (arc) motion swivelled around the elbow or shoulder

TETTSUI UCHI
HAMMER STRIKE

NUKITE
SPEAR HAND STRIKE

URAKEN
BACK FIST STRIKE

SHUTO UCHI
SWORD HAND STRIKE

TEISHO
PALM STRIKE

HAITO UCHI
RIDGE HAND STRIKE

EMPI UCHI
ELBOW STRIKE

TETTSUI UCHI - HAMMER FIST

打 UCHI WAZA - STRIKES

Several strikes and punches are used for both, blocks and strikes and vice versa. Usually your hip position is in 'hanmi' in defence and 'shomen' in offence.

URAKEN
BACK FIST STRIKE

URAKEN
BACK FIST STRIKE

TEISHO
PALM STRIKE

TETTSUI UCHI
HAMMER STRIKE

打 UCHI WAZA - STRIKES

MAE EMPI UCHI
FRONT ELBOW STRIKE

YOKO EMPI UCHI
SIDE ELBOW STRIKE

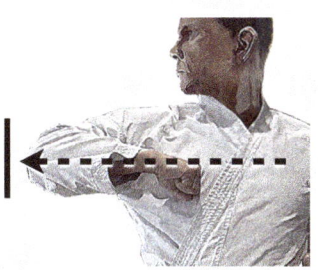

NUKITE
SPEAR HAND STRIKE

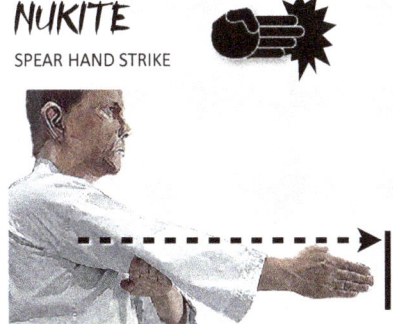

SHUTO UCHI
SWORD/ KNIFE HAND STRIKE

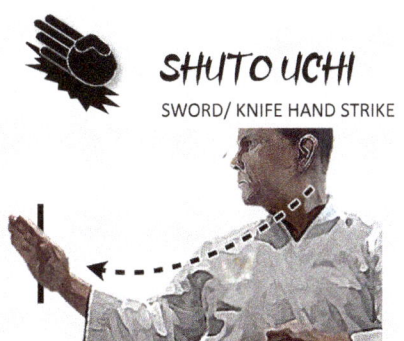

TSUKI & UCHI WAZA

LEARNING PLAN

FORM A FIST (KEN)	TETTSUI UCHI
HIKITE	NUKITE
CHOKU ZUKI	SHUTO UCHI
GYAKU ZUKI	HAITO UCHI
KIZAME	TEISHO UCHI
OI-ZUKI	EMPI UCHI
KAGE ZUKI	AGE ZUKI
URAKEN	SANBON ZUKI - (KIZAME + GYAKU + CHOKU ZUKI)

KERI WAZA - KICKS

Karate has a very high emphasis on the 'grounded' stability and balance for the obvious reasons. This is highlighted and very important to understand with the kicking techniques. Poorly balanced or badly executed kicks have no use in martial arts or sports. They risk an injury and will place you in disadvantage with any opponent, in any situation.

When learning and practising a kick, learn to control the complete technique perfectly in a slow-motion without losing your balance, and keep in mind that 'High' in a kick does not equal good or effective. Start from the lower level kicks and work your way up slowly as you get stronger, gain more muscle control, and master the techniques. A controlled repetition is the best way to develop the correct muscles and muscle groups that are needed to support the techniques and able you to deliver effective kicks.

Don't short-cut your way into higher kicks by forcing them with speed and momentum, this will likely result in an injury and will only result in ineffective, poorly executed, and technically wrong kicks. To be able to perform and deliver powerful and effective kicks takes time and requires lots of practise and repetition. In the end, the hard work will pay off. Keep in mind that using the correct techniques will allow anyone within 'average range of flexibility to learn, perform and deliver these kicks effectively.

踢 KERI WAZA - KICKS

MAE-GERI
FRONT KICK.

Extremely fast straight forward snap-kick delivered with the ball of the foot (Koshi) using either your back or the front foot (Kizame-Geri). Stand in a Zenkutsu Dachi. Maintain your height and the front knee angle. Keep your shoulders and hips squared to the front and your elbows close to your body. Keep your supporting foot firmly anchored to the ground with its toes pointing forward or slightly outwards.

'Slingshot' your foot in a straight ascending line from the floor towards the target by first raising the knee of your fully bent leg up and pointed directly to the target. Then, 'together with thrusting your hips forward, slingshot the leg open and fly the ball of the foot in an explosive, straight motion to the target. And, as quickly, snap it back. (Keep the toes curled up on the kicking foot).

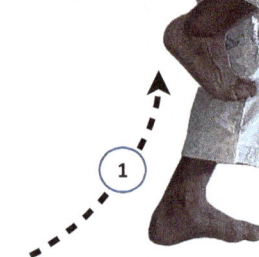

MAE GERI

KERI WAZA - KICKS

MAE-GERI
FRONT KICK.

Emphasise thrusting your hips forward with the kick and strongly pushing forward with the back leg from ground up

MAE GERI

KERI WAZA - KICKS

MAWASHI - GERI

ROUND HOUSE KICK (front or back foot).

Fast and powerful 'circular kick' using hips, body rotation, and a 'slingshot' motion to generate speed and power. This kick is delivered either with the ball, or with top of the foot. (The top of the foot is used in sparring and competitions for safety reasons).

1. In a front stance, maintain your height and the front knee angle. Face forward with your hips and shoulders squared to the front. Lift and level your fully bent leg up to your side at the waist height or higher. Imagine lifting your knee to mount a bicycle. Your weight and your centre of gravity now firmly balanced on the front foot. 2. In one motion, leading with the bent knee, pivot your body sideways with the knee aimed directly to the target. 3. Without stopping the momentum from turning, 'slingshot' the chambered leg open in a 'hay cutting' motion and fly the foot to the target. And as quickly, snap it back. (Ensure your knee does not travel across your body / pass the target line).

MAWASHI GERI

KERI WAZA - KICKS

MAWASHI - GERI
ROUND HOUSE KICK (front or back foot).

Emphasise strongly pivoting your hips and body around to power the kick and snapping the leg open.

MAWASHI GERI

踢 KERI WAZA - KICKS

YOKO-GERI-KEAGE
SIDE SNAP KICK (UPWARD MOTION TO THE SIDE).

Uses the outer side of the foot (Sokuto). Start by transferring your weight to one foot and stand (balanced) on it with a slightly bent knee. Keep your weight low and the knee bent to allow adequate hip and joint movement.

1. Slide the kicking foot up against the supporting leg and either rest its outer edge (Sokuto) horisontally on the supporting knee or rest the top of the foot behind your supporting knee, above the heel). Keep the knee of the kicking leg (Hiza) pointing towards the target on your side and the supporting leg slightly bent.

YOKO GERI KEAGE

KERI WAZA - KICKS

YOKO-GERI-KEAGE
SIDE SNAP KICK (UPWARD MOTION TO THE SIDE).

2. Keep your shoulders slightly rotated backwards and look over the shoulder to the target. From here, bring your knee as high up as you can to your side by rocking your hips upwards to your side. 3. Slingshot the leg open and fly the (horisontally levelled) outer edge of the foot upwards under the target and as quickly snap it back. (Keep the edge of the foot horisontal and don't allow the toes of the kicking foot to rise above the heel.

Ultra fast snap kick directed 'under the target' in upwards circular motion hinged from the knee. Emphasise thrusting the hips and knee upwards to the side.

YOKO GERI KEAGE

KERI WAZA - KICKS

YOKO-GERI- KEKOMI
SIDE THRUST KICK (IN STRAIGHT LINE)

One of the most powerful kicks in any Martial Arts. Delivered with the heel or the bottom of your foot. Imagine stomping and breaking a branch lying on the ground but, doing it sideways. 1. Bring the knee of your chambered leg high up and across your chest. 2. Leading with the knee, pivot your hips around and bring the chambered leg on a horizontal plane to the opposite side of your body at the belt level. The bottom of your foot should now be aimed directly at the target. 3. Extend and 'thrust' your leg to shoot the foot in one straight explosive motion to the target. (Imagine breaking that branch). And as quickly snap it back.

YOKO GERI KEKOMI

KERI WAZA - KICKS

YOKO-GERI-KEKOMI
SIDE THRUST KICK (FROM FRONT STANCE)

Emphasise thrusting your whole body forward with the kick and strongly pushing it forward with the back leg.

YOKO GERI KEKOMI
YOKO GERI KEKOMI

KERI WAZA - KICKS

YOKO-GERI-KEKOMI
SIDE THRUST KICK (FROM SIDE STANCE)

Kekomi from Kiba Dachi

USHIRO – GERI
BACKWARDS KICK

Another powerful kick. Imagine kicking backwards with your heel like a horse. To start, stand in a front stance, maintain your height and bring your front knee in, up and close to your body. Transfer your weight and centre of your gravity on your back foot. Then thrust and drive your heel (toes down) straight backwards in an explosive motion directly to the target behind you. And as quickly, snap it back.

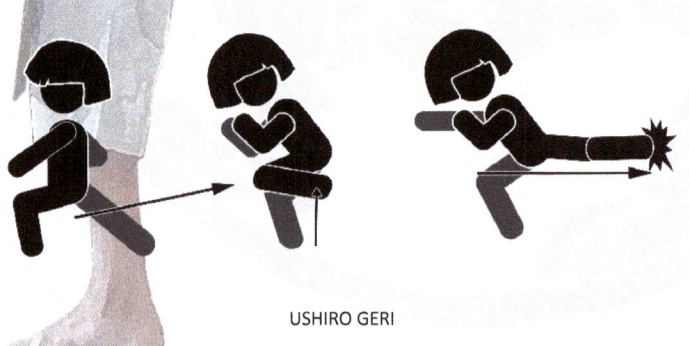

USHIRO GERI

KERI WAZA - KICKS

FUMIKOMI - GERI
STOMP KICK

Stomping kick, the name says it all. Imagine breaking a branch of a tree that is lying on the ground. Lift your knee up and stomp your flat foot or the heel to crush the target.

FUMIKOMI - GERI

Worth to research: Mikazuki-Geri, Hiza-Geri, Nami-Gaeshi, Ura-Mawashi-Geri, Ashi Barai and Mae-Tobi-Geri.

KERI WAZA - KICKS

LEARNING PLAN

MAE GERI	NAMI GAESHI
MAWASHI GERI	URA MAWASHI GERI
YOKO GERI KEKOMI	
YOKO GERI KEAGE	
USHIRO GERI	
FUMIKOMI GERI	
MIKAZUKI GERI	
HIZA GERI	

KIHON - BASICS TRAINING

KIHON / IDO KIHON

Moving basics - Beginner Blocks and Punches (No partner)

START FROM YOI (HEIKO DACHI)

1. STEP FORWARD TO LH FRONT STANCE (ZENKUTSU-DACHI). BLOCK LH LOWER BLOCK (GEDAN-BARAI), PUNCH RH REVERSE PUNCH (GYAKU-ZUKI)

2. STEP FORWARD TO RH FRONT STANCE (ZENKUTSU-DACHI). BLOCK RH AGE-UKE, PUNCH LH REVERSE PUNCH (GYAKU-ZUKI)

3. STEP FORWARD TO LH FRONT STANCE (ZENKUTSU-DACHI). BLOCK LH SOTO-UKE, PUNCH RH REVERSE PUNCH (GYAKU-ZUKI)

4. STEP BACKWARDS TO RH FRONT STANCE (ZENKUTSU-DACHI). BLOCK RH UCHI UKE, PUNCH LH REVERSE PUNCH (GYAKU-ZUKI)

5. STEP FORWARD TO LH BACK STANCE (KOKUTSU-DACHI), BLOCK LH KNIFE HAND BLOCK (SHUTO-UKE),

6. CHANGE LEGS ON A SPOT TO RH BACK STANCE (KOKUTSU-DACHI), BLOCK RH KNIFE HAND BLOCK (SHUTO-UKE),

7. CHANGE STANCE TO LH FRONT STANCE (ZENKUTSU-DACHI). STRIKE LH SPEAR HAND STRIKE (NUKITE)

MAWATTE - TURN AROUND AND REPEAT STARTING WITH RH SIDE

KIHON - BASICS TRAINING

KIHON / IDO KIHON
Moving basics - Intermediate Kicks (No partner)

1. TAKE FORWARD LH FIGHT STANCE

2. (REN-GERI) KICK CHUDAN MAE-GERI WITH A FRONT LEG ON A SPOT. STEP THROUGH AND KICK JODAN MAE-GERI WITH THE BACK LEG (RIGHT LEG). THIS COMBINATION IS CALLED REN-GERI

3. STEP THROUGH AND KICK MAWASHI-GERI WITH RIGHT LEG

4. LAND BACK TO FRONT, FEET TOGETHER AND KICK USHIRO-GERI

5. TURN AND LAND IN ZENKUTSU DACHI

KIHON / IDO KIHON
Moving basics - Intermediate Side Kicks

1. STEP FORWARD WITH LEFT LEG TO LH KIBA DACHI.

2. STEP THROUGH TO LEFT AND KICK LH YOKO-GERI-KEAGE (IN KIBA-DACHI)

3. STEP THROUGH TO RIGHT AND KICK RH YOKO-GERI-KEAGE (IN KIBA-DACHI)

4. STEP THROUGH TO LEFT AND KICK LH YOKO-GERI-KEKOMI (IN KIBA-DACHI) WITHOUT STOPPING FOLLOW WITH STEP THROUGH AND LH YOKO-GERI-KEAGE (IN KIBA-DACHI)

5. STEP THROUGH TO RIGHT AND KICK RH YOKO-GERI-KEKOMI (IN KIBA-DACHI) WITHOUT STOPPING FOLLOW WITH STEP THROUGH AND RH YOKO-GERI-KEAGE (IN KIBA-DACHI)

KIHON - BASICS TRAINING

KIHON / IDO KIHON

Moving basics - Advanced (No partner)

1. STEP FORWARD ZENKUTSU-DACHI. PUNCH SANBON-ZUKI. (KIZAME - GYUAKU-CHOKU ZUKI)

2. STEP BACK TO ZENKUTSU-DACHI. BLOCK AGE-UKE, PUNCH GYAKU-ZUKI

3. STEP FORWARD TO ZENKUTSU-DACHI. BLOCK SOTO-UKE,

4. CHANGE STANCE TO KIBA-DACHI. STRIKE YOKO-ENPI + YOKO-URAKEN UCHI,

5. CHANGE STANCE TO ZENKUTSU-DACHI. PUNCH GYAKU-ZUKI

6. STEP BACK TO ZENKUTSU-DACHI. BLOCK UCHI-UKE, PUNCH KIZAME AND GYAKU-ZUKI.

7. STEP FORWARD TO KOKUTSU-DACHI, BLOCK SHUTO-UKE,

7.1 CHANGE STANCE TO ZENKUTSU-DACHI. STRIKE NUKITE

8. KICK MAE-GERI ON FRONT LEG (on the spot),

7.2 CHANGE BACK TO KOKUTSU-DACHI, BLOCK SHUTO-UKE,

8. (REN-GERI) KICK CHUDAN MAE-GERI ON FRONT LEG (on the spot), STEP IN AND KICK JODAN MAE-GERI THROUGH WITH THE BACK LEG. (LAND IN ZENKUTSU-DACHI)

9. STEP IN AND KICK MAWASHI-GERI THROUGH WITH THE BACK LEG. (LAND IN KIBA-DACHI)

10. STEP THROUGH IN KIBA DACHI AND KICK YOKO-GERI-KEAGE (LEFT AND RIGHT SIDE)

11. FINISH WITH YOKO GERI KEKOMI (STEP THROUGH WITH ZENKUTSU DACHI)

KUMITE - SPARRING

The One-, Three- and Five-Step kumite drills are a 'controlled simulated fighting environment' where we test, practise, develop and improve our (Kihon) skills and techniques against a real person and learn to adjust, manipulate, and control the critical aspects of our defences (Distance, Block) and offences (Balance, Distance, Timing and Accuracy) in a real time. The Jiyu-Ippon (Semi-free) and the Jiyu (Free) kumite are for pressure testing and improving those skills at the higher level.

TARGET LEVELS

For the purpose of the learning exercise in hand, clarity and safety, we inform our training partners clearly on our intended target levels and techniques. This will allow our partners to prepare and fully focus on learning the right technique.

'JODAN –   UPPER LEVEL
Above the neck. E.g. Block a Jodan punch with Age Uke

'CHUDAN - MID LEVEL
Above the belt E.g. Block a Chudan Punch with a Soto Uke or a Mawashi-Geri with a Uchi-Uke

'GEDAN   LOWER LEVEL
Under the belt E.g. Block a Mae Geri with Gedan Barai

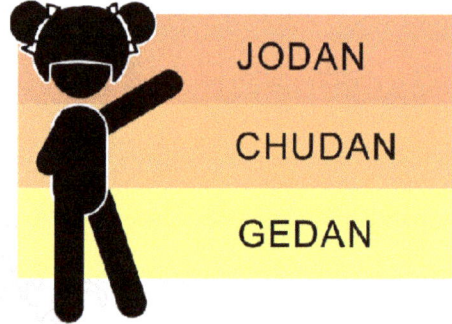

KUMITE - SPARRING

IPPON KUMITE - ONE STEP
ONE STEP SPARRING DRILL WITH A PARTNER

Sensei will set up your routine and determine what techniques are practised and in what order. You will line up, face, and greet your partner by bowing in Musubi Dachi and take a Heiko Dachi ready stance ('YOI').

The person attacking starts by taking a step backwards into Zenkutsu Dachi at the striking distance. They clearly inform their partner of the technique they are going to use and their intended 'target', (Jodan punch, chudan punch, or a kick). Then, with a forward step, they will deliver their technique (Punch or Kick) as close to the target (E.g. Philtrum) as is considered safe and a requirement at their belt grade. When stepping forward, move in a straight line and step near or next to the 'insole' of your partner's front foot. (Not on their toes!). It is important to deliver your punch (or kick) with an intent to reach the target. Otherwise, the opportunity to learn will be lost to both of you.

Person defending will response to the attack by stepping backwards into relevant defensive stance (E.g. Zenkutsu Dachi) and using the relevant defensive technique (E.g. Age-Uke) to block the attack, then perform a counter strike with 'Kiai'. (E.g. Gyaku Zuki). When stepping backwards you will need to step far enough to avoid the punch but, stay close enough (at striking distance) to be able to deliver a counter strike.

Once the drill is over, or when changing partners, you should thank your current partner (and welcome the new one) with a bow.

When moving backwards, pay extra attention where and how you place your back foot. How far and how wide will determine how effectively you can block, counter strike, maintain your balance or move again.

KUMITE - SPARRING

IPPON KUMITE - ONE STEP
ONE STEP SPARRING DRILL WITH A PARTNER

In sparring we **KIAI** on start, delivery and counter punch.

- When moving backwards, pay extra attention where and how you place your back foot. How far and how wide will determine how effectively you can block, counter strike and maintain your balance or move again.

When changing positions between the stances, pay extra attention where your centre of gravity is and the weight distribution for good balance (e.g weight from front to bag leg or evenly to both like in kiba dachi).

KUMITE - SPARRING

GOHON KUMITE

5-STEP SPARRING DRILL WITH A PARTNER.

In five-step sparring you work exactly as in Ippon Kumite, but the person attacking will deliver the same technique consecutively 5 times in a row stepping forward and stopping each time, 'Kiai' only on the last one. The Person defending will response and step backwards in a straight line for those 5 times and only deliver the counter strike with a 'Kiai' on the last one. Then, you will reverse your roles and work your way back to the start.

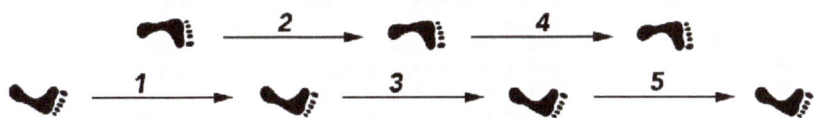

JIYU IPPON KUMITE

SEMI-FREE ONE-STEP SPARRING WITH A PARTNER

As in 'Ippon Kumite' with the set techniques, 'one strike and one response' at the time, but both 'opponents' (training partners) are moving freely in their 'Kamae' (fighting stance) and deliver their techniques and respond to attacks in 'real time' in a more realistic scenario. Purpose of this training is to condition ourselves (mentally and physically), and to adjust our speed, balance, accuracy, and distance to work in real-life scenarios and in competition environment. Next level up from here is the **JIYU Kumite**, free fighting kumite with no set techniques or any advanced notice for techniques used.

IPPON KUMITE

LEARNING PLAN

ATTACKER	STEP FORWARD TO RH UPPER PUNCH (JODAN OI-ZUKI OR KIZAME)
DEFENDER	STEP BACK TO LH UPPER BLOCK (AGE-UKE) & RH MID LEVEL REVERSE COUNTER PUNCH (CHUDAN GYAKU-ZUKI)
ATTACKER	STEP FORWARD TO RH MID LEVEL PUNCH (CHUDAN OI-ZUKI)
DEFENDER	STEP BACK TO LH MID LEVEL OUTER BLOCK (CHUDAN SOTO UKE) & RH MID LEVEL REVERSE COUNTER PUNCH (CHUDAN GYAKU-ZUKI)
ATTACKER	STEP FORWARD TO RH MID LEVEL FRONT KICK (CHUDAN MAE GERI)
DEFENDER	TAKE A RIGHT SHIFT BACK STEP (TAI SABAKI) TO LH LOWER BLOCK (GEDAN BARAI) & RH REVERSE COUNTER PUNCH (CHUDAN GYAKU-ZUKI)
ATTACKER	STEP FORWARD TO RH SIDE THRUST KICK (YOKO GERI KEKOMI)
DEFENDER	TAKE A LEFT SHIFT BACK STEP (TAI SABAKI) TO LH OUTER BLOCK (SOTO-UKE)
ATTACKER	STEP FORWARD TO RH ROUNDHOUSE KICK (MAWASHI GERI)
DEFENDER	TAKE A RIGHT SHIFT BACK STEP (TAI SABAKI) TO - LH INSIDE BLOCK (UCHI UKE)

Key words, Offence: Balance, Distance, Timing, and Accuracy.
Defence: Adequate Distance, Block

IPPON KUMITE

LEARNING PLAN

In this one step kumite exercise all the blocks are done with the same hand and stepped back with the same leg. Then repeated on the other side

1. JODAN OI-ZUKI & AGE-UKE

2. CHUDAN OI-ZUKI & SOTO-UKE

3. CHUDAN MAE GERI & GEDAN BARAI

IPPON KUMITE

LEARNING PLAN

Defender's emphasis on balance, stability and distance. Placing the back foot on right distance to allow safe, effective blocking and reaching the opponent with the counter strikes. Attacker's emphasis on accuracy, balance, timing and distance

4. YOKO GERI KEKOMI & SOTO-UKE

5. MAWASHI GERI & UCHI UKE

KATA PATTERNS

Purpose of Kata

'Katas' are one of the three pillars of Karate training and learning. Kihon, Kata and Kumite. Katas are not a dance or a theatrical performance. They are practised and trained as used in a realistic fighting. While performing or practising a Kata you will need to apply serious concentration, strength, power, and speed. Your Kata techniques must reflect their true impact to the opponent, as in fight application.

Katas combine our stances and footwork with the other techniques and places them in a predetermined 'Fight-Simulation' where the imagined 'threats', their direction, nature and required 'responses' changes almost with each step taken. Lower-level Katas start with the most basic moves, but are by no means less effective (rather the opposite) than the higher-level Katas that require much more experience, technical skills and further knowledge to perform correctly.

Katas provide us a platform and a practise ground for a vast number of variations and combinations that strengthen, condition and improve our mental and physical abilities to response effectively in variable situations. Katas are also used as a 'benchmark' and a tool to test, review and showcase our skill levels and abilities.

With Katas, we train and learn to shift our focus, change of direction, control timing, quick and slow movements, shifting from extreme acceleration to fully controlled stops and from high jumps to 'slow-motion' techniques. We learn control, stability and balancing in high and low stances. We learn to deliver powerful and explosive techniques with 'Kime'.

When you get on that floor to perform your Kata, do your best, thrive to your best performance and deliver your every move with a real intent every time, and don't hold back just because you are afraid of making a mistake or afraid to fail. Mistakes do happen, we learn from them, they make us work harder and in the end, they make us better and stronger. Take your strongest ready stance, put your warrior face on and have a go at it.

 # KATA PATTERNS

Performing Kata

Bow before stepping on to the mat. Walk in a centre front of the mat, face and bow to the front, then to your opponent (if applicable). Hold your head high, eyes up and walk confidently on the mat, directly to your starting spot, and take a Musubi Dachi stance. Next, make a calm and respectful bow to the front, stand up and strongly shout out your Kata name. Then take a confident 'Yoi' stance (Heiko Dachi) and start the kata moves. At the end, after your last move, retract back to your 'Yoi' stance in a strong and controlled fashion facing the front again. Take a Musubi Dachi stance, bow and retract out from the mat

- Kata starts and ends with a bow (Rei). (Failing to bow first can lead to disqualification)
- Kata starts and finishes at the same exact spot.
- The first move in each kata is a block, ("There is no first strike in Karate").

Always keep an upright posture and maintain your head height throughout the Kata, unless a specific technique requires you to do something else, like jumping or kneeling etc. Pay attention to your breathing, its timing and rhythm and ensure your slow and fast movements are clearly distinguishable as 'slow' and 'fast'. Ensure the fast and quick moves are fully completed, don't shortcut a move to be quicker or faster. When performing a move or a technique, do it with its 'real intent' and pay extra attention to your balance.

Learn and understand the purpose of your Katas. Katas are not just for a show. Think, what is the main purpose of each move and the intent of each technique? How can I make them effective in a real life scenario? This will help you to remember and perform your kata much better.

Know your Kata, when you don't, it shows.

KATA PATTERNS

Competition Criteria for evaluation. Kata Performance

Technical performance (70%)

a. Stances
b. Techniques
c. Transitional movements
d. Timing e. Correct breathing
f. Focus (KIME)
g. Consistence in the performance of the KIHON of the style in the kata.

2. Athletic performance (30%)
a. Strength
b. Speed
c. Balance

Assessment

Kata is not a dance or theatrical performance. It must adhere to the traditional values and principles. It must be realistic in fighting terms and display concentration, power, and potential impact in its techniques. It must demonstrate strength, power, and speed — as well as grace, rhythm, and balance

In assessing the performance of a Competitor or team, the Judges will evaluate the performance based on the two major criteria (technical performance 70% and athletic performance 30%).

The performance is evaluated from the bow starting the kata until the bow ending the kata with the exception of team medal matches, where the performance, as well as the timekeeping starts at the bow in the beginning of the kata and ends when the performers bow after completing the Bunkai. Slight variation as taught by the Competitor's style (Ryu- Ha) of Karate will be permitted.

KATA PATTERNS

Our recommended order of learning Katas. (Per Kyu level)

TAIKYOKU SHODAN	10-9 Kyu
JO NO	9-8 Kyu
HEIAN SHODAN	9-8 Kyu
HEIAN NIDAN	8-7 Kyu
HEIAN SANDAN	7-6 Kyu
HEIAN YONDAN	6-5 Kyu
HEIAN GODAN	5-4 Kyu
TEKKI SHODAN	4-3 Kyu
BASSAI DAI	3-1 Kyu to 1 Dan
JION	3-1 Kyu to 1 Dan
EMPI	3-1 Kyu to 1 Dan
KANKU DAI	3-1 Kyu to 1 Dan

*KIME! A focus point. The moment of controlled delivery and completion of any Karate technique to its maximum impact and power. The Muscle 'power' contraction point, 'Relaxed, Contracted, Relaxed'. the "100" in "0-100-0".

*KIAI! Is the name of our 'battle cry' or a short 'shout out', to assist us releasing the full power of our 'Kime' in our Kihon, Kata and Kumite training. We are not actually saying 'Kiai. Have a go, don't hold back and try it with your punch! (Hi-yah!, Aiyah!, Eeee-yah! or Hyah!').

# KATA PATTERNS

KEY POINTS IN KATA PERFORMANCE

- **Stances** - Size, foot positioning, knee and foot angles and orientation, weight distribution, balance, stability, height, and posture.
- **Techniques**' – Correct, complete, effective for their intended purpose and target, speed, distance, accuracy, strength and 'kime'
- **Transitional movements** – Control, balance, stability, weight transfer and distribution, speed, height, posture and foot position.
- **Timing** – Correct rhythm and flow with clearly completed techniques, transitions and stops. Clear distinction between the slow and fast movements. The total time taken to finish.
- **Breathing** – Correct breathing technique. Timing of inhaling/ out haling when completing a technique.
- **Focus** (KIME) – Strength and ability to control and deliver techniques with Kime 0-100-0.
- Using the **actual movements** as intended in the kata.

- **Strength**
- **Speed**
- **Balance**
- **Knowledge –** Know your Kata. Have a clear idea and intention for the moves you perform, when you don't, it shows.

EMBUSEN

The 'shape' or the 'path' Kata follows

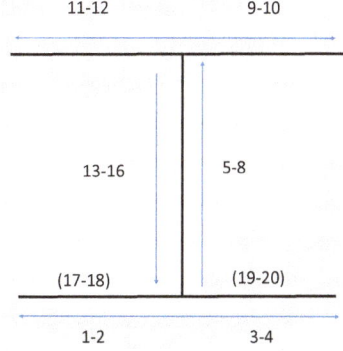

KATA PATTERNS

SHOTOKAN KATA LIST FOR COMPETITIONS

HEIAN KATA
Heian Shodan
Heian Nidan
Heian Sandan
Heian Yondan
Heian Godan

TEKKI
Tekki Shodan
Tekki Nidan
Tekki Sandan

ADVANCED KATA
(Listed by Masatoshi Nakayama)
Kanku Sho
Bassai Sho
Chinte
Nijushiho
Sochin
Unsu (Considered most advanced)
Gojushiho Sho
Gojushiho Dai
Meikyo

SENTEI KATA
Bassai Dai
Kanku Dai
Jion
Empi

ADVANCED KATA
(Tought by Gichin Funakoshi)
Jitte
Gankaku
Hangetsu

ADVANCED KATA
(Rare)
Wankan
Jiin

KATA PATTERNS

LEARNING PLAN

TAIKYOKU SHODAN	BASSAI DAI
JO NO	EMPI
HEIAN SHODAN	JION
HEIAN NIDAN	KANKU DAI
HEIAN SANDAN	
HEIAN YONDAN	
HEIAN GODAN	
TEKKI SHODAN	

TAIKYOKU SHODAN

The 'Ultimate First' Kata

Our first and most basic Kata with only two hand techniques, the Lower Block and Trough Punch, (Gedan Barai + Oi-Zuki). In total it has twenty moves, which are all performed in a front stance (Zenkutsu Dachi). We Learn to use our 90° Left-Turns, 180° Right D-Turns, and 270° Around the back-Turns to the left. All the turns lead to down block (Gedan Barai) and all the forward steps are performed with the 'step through' punch, (Oi-zuki).

Name	**TAIKYOKU SHODAN – 'ULTIMATE FIRST LEVEL'**
Moves	20
KIAI	8 & 16
Techniques	Lower block (GEDAN BARAI), Through Punch (OI-ZUKI)
Stances	Zenkutsu Dachi

EMBUSEN

The 'shape' or the 'path' Kata follows

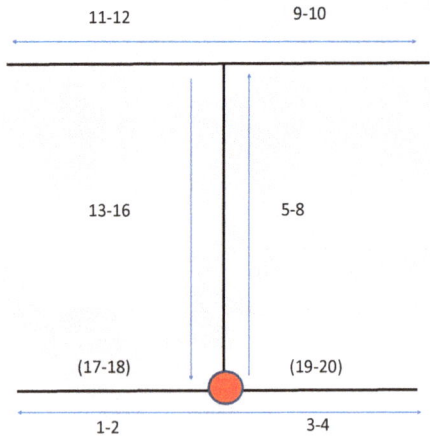

型 TAIKYOKU SHODAN

 90° LH

 180° RH

 90° LH

 270° LH

 180° RH

 90° LH

 270° LH

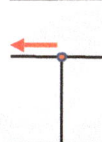 180° RH

1
LH GEDAN BARAI
LH ZENKUTSU DACHI

2
RH CHUDAN OI-ZUKI
RH ZENKUTSU DACHI

3
RH GEDAN BARAI
RH ZENKUTSU DACHI

4
LH CHUDAN OI-ZUKI
LH ZENKUTSU DACHI

5
LH GEDAN BARAI
LH ZENKUTSU DACHI

6 / 7 / 8  KIAI !!!
6: RH / RH
7: + LH / + LH
8: + RH CHUDAN OI-ZUKI / + RH ZENKUTSU DACHI

9
LH GEDAN BARAI
LH ZENKUTSU DACHI

10
RH CHUDAN OI-ZUKI
RH ZENKUTSU DACHI

11
RH GEDAN BARAI
RH ZENKUTSU DACHI

12
LH CHUDAN OI-ZUKI
LH ZENKUTSU DACHI

13
LH GEDAN BARAI
LH ZENKUTSU DACHI

14 / 15 / 16  KIAI !!!
14: RH / RH
15: + LH / + LH
16: + RH OI-ZUKI / + RH ZENKUTSU DACHI

17
LH GEDAN BARAI
LH ZENKUTSU DACHI

18
RH CHUDAN OI-ZUKI
RH ZENKUTSU DACHI

19
RH GEDAN BARAI
RH ZENKUTSU DACHI

20
LH CHUDAN OI-ZUKI
LH ZENKUTSU DACHI

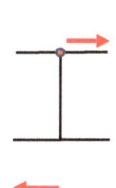
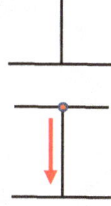

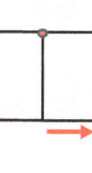

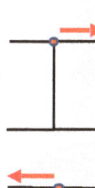

JO NO

Our second Kata introduces us Jodan and Chudan level blocking with Age-Uke and Soto-Uke. It also introduces the front kick, Mae-Geri, and the two Knife-hand blocks Shuto-Uke and Tate-Shuto-Uke (Vertical Knife-hand block). When performing steps 17-19, pay extra attention to how you transition your centre of gravity between the stances, and make sure you have clearly distinguishable 'slow and fast' moves.

Name	JO NO
Moves	21
KIAI	8 & 21
Techniques	Lower block (Gedan Barai), Upper Block (Age-Uke), Through Punch (Oi-Zuki), Outer Block (Soto-Uke), Front Kick (Mae-Geri), Knife Hand Block (Shuto-Uke), (Vertical) Tate-Shuto-Uke, Front Punch (Choku-Zuki).
Stances	Zenkutsu Dachi, Kokutsu Dachi, Kiba Dachi

EMBUSEN

The 'shape' or the 'path' Kata follows

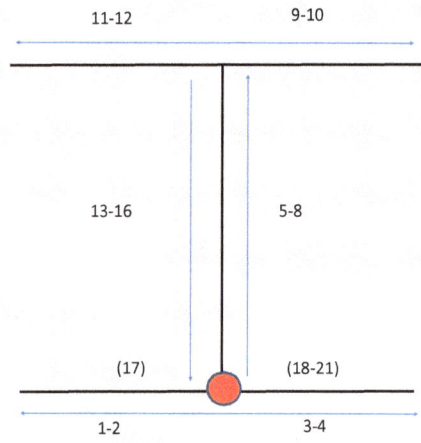

JO NO

Turn	#	Technique	Stance
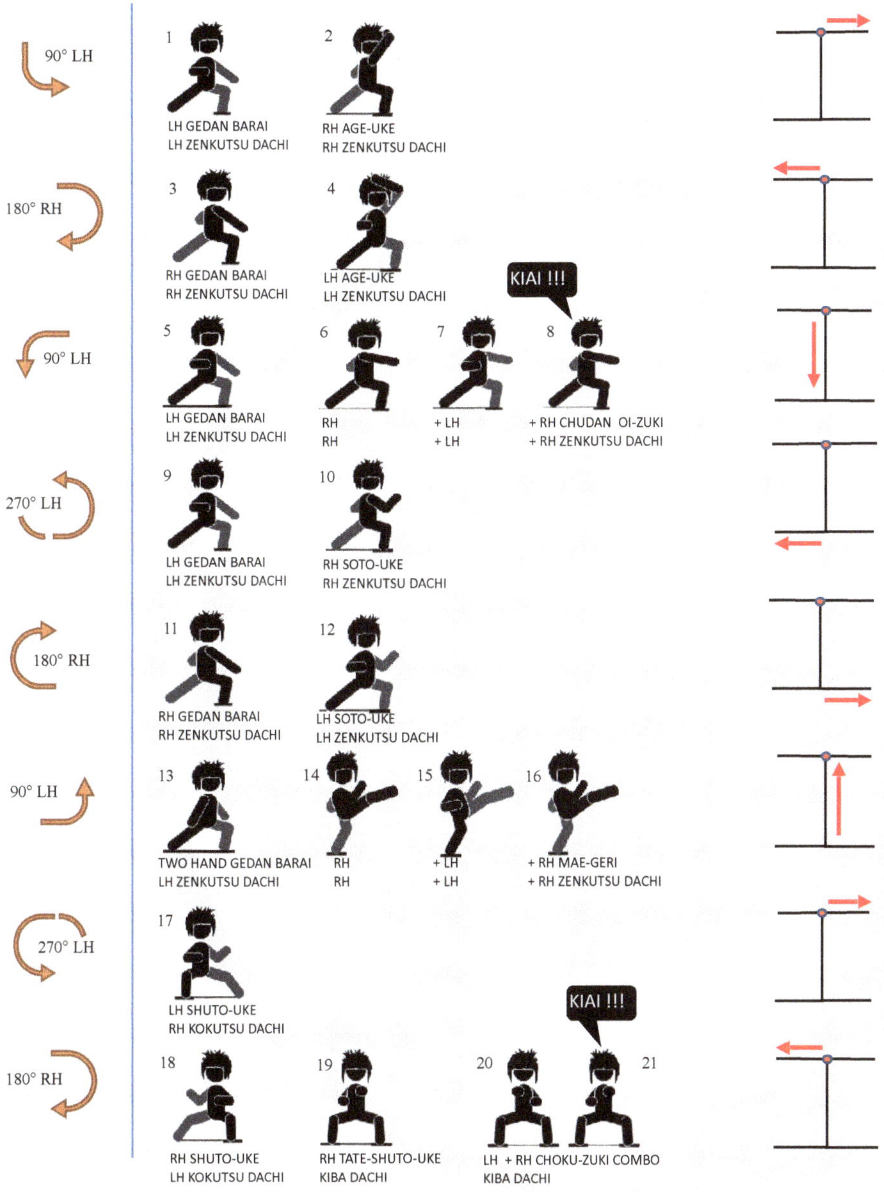 90° LH	1	LH GEDAN BARAI	LH ZENKUTSU DACHI
	2	RH AGE-UKE	RH ZENKUTSU DACHI
180° RH	3	RH GEDAN BARAI	RH ZENKUTSU DACHI
	4	LH AGE-UKE	LH ZENKUTSU DACHI
90° LH	5	LH GEDAN BARAI	LH ZENKUTSU DACHI
	6	RH	RH
	7	+ LH	+ LH
	8	+ RH CHUDAN OI-ZUKI — KIAI !!!	+ RH ZENKUTSU DACHI
270° LH	9	LH GEDAN BARAI	LH ZENKUTSU DACHI
	10	RH SOTO-UKE	RH ZENKUTSU DACHI
180° RH	11	RH GEDAN BARAI	RH ZENKUTSU DACHI
	12	LH SOTO-UKE	LH ZENKUTSU DACHI
90° LH	13	TWO HAND GEDAN BARAI	LH ZENKUTSU DACHI
	14	RH	RH
	15	+ LH	+ LH
	16	+ RH MAE-GERI	+ RH ZENKUTSU DACHI
270° LH	17	LH SHUTO-UKE	RH KOKUTSU DACHI
180° RH	18	RH SHUTO-UKE	LH KOKUTSU DACHI
	19	RH TATE-SHUTO-UKE	KIBA DACHI
	20-21	LH + RH CHOKU-ZUKI COMBO — KIAI !!!	KIBA DACHI

HEIAN SHODAN

First of the five Heian 'The Peaceful Mind' Katas with twenty one moves. It introduces us to Gedan-Barai, Oi-Zuki, Tettsui Uchi ('Hammer fist Strike'), and Age-Uke performed in Zenkutsu Dachi, and to Shuto-Uke performed in Kokutsu-Dachi with 180, 90 and 45 degree turns.

Name	**HEIAN SHODAN,** 'THE PEACEFUL MIND' FIRST LEVEL
Moves	21
KIAI	9 & 17
Techniques	Lower block (Gedan Barai), Through Punch (Oi-Zuki), Hammer Fist Strike (Tettsui-Uchi), Upper Block (Age-Uke), Knife Hand Block (Shuto-Uke)
Stances	Zenkutsu Dachi, Kokutsu Dachi.

EMBUSEN

The 'shape' or the 'path' Kata follows

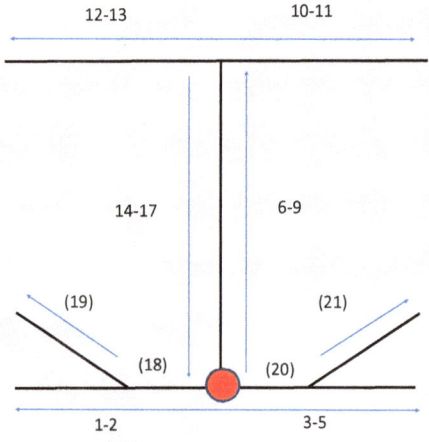

HEIAN SHODAN

 90° LH

 180° RH

 90° LH

 270° LH

 180° RH

 90° LH

 270° LH

 180° RH

1.  LH GEDAN BARAI / LH ZENKUTSU DACHI
2.  RH CHUDAN OI-ZUKI / RH ZENKUTSU DACHI
3.  RH GEDAN BARAI / RH ZENKUTSU DACHI
4.  RH TETTSUI UCHI / RH SHO-ZENKUTSU
5.  LH CHUDAN OI-ZUKI / LH ZENKUTSU DACHI
6.  LH GEDAN BARAI / LH ZENKUTSU DACHI
7.  RH / RH
8.  + LH / + LH
9.  KIAI! + RH AGE-UKE / + RH ZENKUTSU DACHI
10.  LH GEDAN BARAI / LH ZENKUTSU DACHI
11.  RH CHUDAN OI-ZUKI / RH ZENKUTSU DACHI
12.  RH GEDAN BARAI / RH ZENKUTSU DACHI
13.  LH CHUDAN OI-ZUKI / LH ZENKUTSU DACHI
14.  LH GEDAN BARAI / LH ZENKUTSU DACHI
15.  RH / RH
16.  + LH / + LH
17.  KIAI! + RH OI-ZUKI / + RH ZENKUTSU DACHI
18.  LH SHUTO-UKE / RH KOKUTSU DACHI
     45° RH
19.  RH SHUTO-UKE / LH KOKUTSU DACHI
20. RH SHUTO-UKE / LH KOKUTSU DACHI
    45° LH
21. HH SHUTO-UKE / RH KOKUTSU DACHI

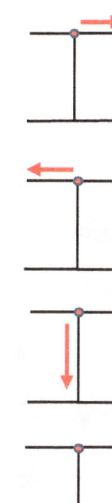

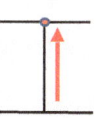

GRADING

CRITERIA

Many different styles and some individual clubs use their own adopted variations of the colours, syllabus and grading criteria to suite their specific ranking systems. Ranks are earned/ achieved through skill assessment and grading tests that are based on a set skill, knowledge, and attendance criterion for each level. During the test students are required to perform and demonstrate a prescribed set of karate techniques in a front of accredited examiners.

When joining a club its best to ensure they are officially recognised under relevant national sporting body and internationally recognised by relevant Karate organisation and authorised to run grading exams.

FOLLOWING SYLLABUS IS ONLY A GENERIC SAMPLE OF WHAT COULD BE EXPECTED FOR DIFFERENT KYU LEVELS.

GRADING SYLLABUS

10-8TH KYU

10th & 9th Kyu (WHITE/ YELLOW WHITE)
BASICS. FROM HEIKO DACHI TO ZENKUTSU DACHI (FRONT STANCE)

CHUDAN CHOKU-ZUKI (FRONT PUNCH)

CHUDAN OI-ZUKI (STEP THROUGH PUNCH)

JODAN AGE-UKE (UPPER BLOCK)

CHUDAN SOTO-UKE BLOCK (FROM OUTSIDE BLOCK)

GEDAN BARAI (LOWER BLOCK)

MAE-GERI KICK (FRONT KICK)

8th Kyu YELLOW

IDO KIHON MOVING BASICS
MOVING IN FRONT AND BACK STANCE

CHUDAN OI-ZUKI (STEP THROUGH PUNCH)

JODAN AGE-UKE BLOCK (UPPER BLOCK)

CHUDAN SOTO-UKE BLOCK (FROM OUTSIDE BLOCK)

GEDAN BARAI (LOWER BLOCK)

IN KOKUTSU DACHI, SHUTO-UKE (KNIFE HAND BLOCK)

MAE-GERI KICK (FRONT KICK)

YOKO-GERI KEAGE (SIDE SNAP KICK)

(KATA)   TAIKYOKU SHODAN

(KUMITE) GOHON 5-STEP KUMITE (JODAN OI-ZUKI, CHUDAN OI-ZUKI)

GRADING SYLLABUS

7-6TH KYU

7th Kyu ORANGE

IDO KIHON MOVING BASICS.
- CHUDAN OI-ZUKI (STEP THROUGH PUNCH) FORWARD
- JODAN AGE-UKE BLOCK BACKWARD
- CHUDAN SOTO-UKE BLOCK FORWARD
- CHUDAN UCHI-UKE BACKWARD
- IN KOKUTSU-DACHI SHUTO-UKE FORWARD
- TURN AROUND, MAE-GERI KICK (FRONT KICK)
- YOKO-GERI KEAGE (MOVING IN KIBA DACHI, (RIGHT AND LEFT)

(KATA)   HEIAN SHODAN
(KUMITE) GOHON 5-STEP KUMITE (JODAN OI-ZUKI, CHUDAN OI-ZUKI)

6th Kyu GREEN

IDO KIHON MOVING BASICS.
- CHUDAN OI-ZUKI (STEP THROUGH PUNCH) FORWARD
- JODAN AGE-UKE BLOCK BACKWARD
- CHUDAN SOTO-UKE BLOCK FORWARD
- CHUDAN UCHI-UKE BACKWARD
- IN KOKUTSU-DACHI SHUTO-UKE FORWARD
- TURN AROUND, MAE-GERI KICK
- YOKO-GERI KEAGE (in KIBA DACHI, RIGHT AND LEFT)
- YOKO-GERI KEKOMI (in KIBA DACHI, RIGHT AND LEFT)

(KATA)   HEIAN NIDAN
(KUMITE) KIHON IPPON ONE STEP KUMITE

GRADING SYLLABUS

5-4TH KYU

5th Kyu BLUE

CHUDAN OI-ZUKI THROUGH PUNCH FORWARD
JODAN AGE-UKE (UPPER BLOCK), GYAKU ZUKI BACKWARD
CHUDAN SOTO-UKE BLOCK, GYAKU ZUKI FORWARD
CHUDAN UCHI-UKE, CHUDAN GYAKU ZUKI BACKWARD
IN KOKUTSU-DACHI SHUTO-UKE FORWARD
TURN AROUND, MAE-GERI KICK
YOKO-GERI KEAGE (in KIBA DACHI, RIGHT AND LEFT)
YOKO-GERI KEKOMI (in KIBA DACHI, RIGHT AND LEFT)
(KATA)   HEIAN SANDAN
(KUMITE) KIHON IPPON KUMITE

4th Kyu PURPLE

CHUDAN OI-ZUKI
JODAN AGE-UKE (UPPER BLOCK), GYAKU ZUKI
CHUDAN SOTO-UKE BLOCK, GYAKU ZUKI
CHUDAN UCHI-UKE, GYAKU ZUKI
IN KOKUTSU-DACHI SHUTO-UKE, ZENKUTSU NUKITE
MAE-GERI KICK
YOKO-GERI KEAGE (in KIBA DACHI, RIGHT AND LEFT)
YOKO-GERI KEKOMI (in KIBA DACHI, RIGHT AND LEFT)
(KATA)   HEIAN YONDAN
(KUMITE) KIHON IPPON KUMITE

GRADING SYLLABUS

3-2ND KYU

3rd Kyu BROWN AND WHITE

CHUDAN OI-ZUKI FORWARDS

JODAN AGE-UKE (UPPER BLOCK), GYAKU-ZUKI

CHUDAN SOTO-UKE BLOCK, GYAKU-ZUKI

CHUDAN UCHI-UKE, GYAKU-ZUKI

IN KOKUTSU-DACHI, SHUTO-UKE, ZENKUTSU NUKITE

TURN AROUND. MAE-GERI

TURN AROUND REN-GERI (GEDAN KAKIWAKE CHUDAN, JODAN)

MAWASHIGERI

YOKO-GERI KEAGE (in KIBA DACHI, RIGHT AND LEFT)

YOKO-GERI KEKOMI (in KIBA DACHI, RIGHT AND LEFT)

(KATA)   HEIAN GODAN

(KUMITE) KIHON IPPON KUMITE

2nd Kyu BROWN AND BLACK

CHUDAN OI-ZUKI FORWARD

JODAN AGE-UKE (UPPER BLOCK), GYAKU ZUKI

CHUDAN SOTO-UKE BLOCK IN ZENKUTSU DACHI,
CHANGE TO KIBA DACHI, YOKO ENPI, YOKO URAKEN UCHI

CHUDAN UCHI-UKE, GYAKU ZUKI

IN KOKUTSU-DACHI SHUTO-UKE, ZENKUTSU NUKITE

MAE-GERI KICK

REN GERI (GEDAN KAKIWAKE, CHUDAN, JOUDAN)

MAWASHI GERI

YOKO-GERI KEAGE (in KIBA DACHI, RIGHT AND LEFT)

YOKO-GERI KEKOMI (in ZENKUTSUDATI)

(KATA)   TEKKI SHODAN

(KUMITE) JIYUU IPPON KUMITE

GRADING SYLLABUS

1ST KYU

1st Kyu BROWN

    CHUDAN OI-ZUKI THROUGH PUNCH

    SANBON RENZUKI

    JODAN AGE-UKE (UPPER BLOCK), GYAKU ZUKI

    CHUDAN SOTO-UKE BLOCK IN ZENKUTSU DACHI,
    CHANGE TO KIBA DACHI, YOKO ENPI, YOKO URAKEN UCHI

    CHUDAN UCHI-UKE, GYAKU ZUKI

    IN KOKUTSU-DACHI SHUTO-UKE, ZENKUTSU NUKITE

    MAE-GERI KICK

    RENGERI (FRONT KICK CHUDAN AND JODAN)

    MAWASHIGERI

    YOKO-GERI KEAGE (in KIBA DACHI, RIGHT AND LEFT)

    YOKO-GERI KEKOMI (ZENKUTSU-DACHI)

(KATA)   BASSAI DAI, KANKU DAI, ENPI or JION

(KUMITE) JIYU IPPON KUMITE

KARATE VOCABULARY

Common Words
Back - Ura
Basics – Kihon
Begin – Hajime
Behind– Ushiro
Belt– Obi
Black Belt Rank – Dan
Bow – Rei
Color Belt Rank – Kyu
Fist – Ken
Focus – Kime
Foot – Ashi
Forward - Mae
Kick – Geri
Kneeling– Seiza
Left – Hidari
Line Up – Seiretsu
Lower Level – Gedan
Main Instructor – Sensei
Meditate – Mokuso
Middle (Stomach Level) – Chudan
Punching Board – Makiwara
Right – Migi
School (Martial Arts) – Dojo
Senior Student/ Instructor – Sempai
Sokumen – Side
Sparring – Kumite
Stance – Dachi
Start - Hajime
Stop – Yame

Shifting - Tai Sabaki (from attack line)
Technique – Waza
To the side - Yoko
Turn Around – Mawatte
Uniform – Gi (Gee)
Upper (Head Level) – Jodan

Stances – (DACHI)
Back Stance – Kokutsu Dachi
Cat Stance – Neko Ashi Dachi
Crane Stance - Tsuru Ashi Dashi
Crossed Feet Stance – Kosa Dachi
Feet Together – Heisoku Dachi
Feet V Shape – Musubi Dachi
Front Stance – Zenkutsu Dachi
Horse Riding Stance – Kiba Dachi
Immovable Stance – Fudo Dachi
Knee bending - Hizakutsu Dachi
Leg Stance- Ashi Dachi
L Stance – Renoji Dachi
Ready Stance – Heiko Dachi
T Stance – Teiji Dachi

KARATE VOCABULARY

Blocks – (UKE)
Augmented Block – Morote Uke
Cross Hand Block – Juji Uke
Inside Block – Uchi Uke
Knife Hand Block – Shuto Uke
Lower Block – Gedan Barai
Outside Block – Soto Uke
Palm Block – Teisho Uke
Rising Block – Age Uke
Wedge Block - Kakiwake

Punches (ZUKI) & Hand/Arm Strikes (UCHI)
Back Fist Strike – Uraken Uchi
Elbow Strike – Empi Uchi
Front Punch – Choku Zuki
Hammer fist – Tettsui Uchi
Hook Punch – Kage Zuki
Knife Hand Strike – Shuto Uchi
Leading Punch – Kizame Zuki
Lunge Punch – Oi Zuki
Mountain Punch – Yama Zuki
Palm Heel Strike – Teisho Uchi
Reverse Punch – Gyaku Zuki
Ridge Hand Strike – Haito Uchi
Rising Punch – Age Zuki
Sanbon Zuki – 3 Punch Combination
Spear Hand Strike – Nukite

Kicks – (GERI)
Back Thrust Kick – Ushiro Geri
Crescent Kick – Mika Zuki Geri
Foot Sweep – Ashi Barai
Front Kick – Mae Geri
Knee Kick – Hiza Geri
Nami Gaeshi – Returning Wave
Roundhouse Kick – Mawashi Geri
Side Snap Kick – Yoko Geri Keage
Side Thrust Kick – Yoko Geri Kekomi
Stomp Kick – Fumikomi Geri

Counting
1 Ichi, 2 Ni, 3 San, 4 Shi, 5 Go,
6 Roku, 7 Sichi, 8 Hachi, 9 Ku, 10 Yu

NIJU KUN

20 Guiding Principles of Karate-DO

by Gichin Funakoshi

- Karate begins and ends with bowing (courtesy and respect).
- There is no first strike in karate, (Karate is for defence).
- Karate stands on a side of justice.
- First know yourself, then know the others.
- Cultivating mind is more important than learning a technique.
- Heart (mind) must be set free.
- Accidents come from carelessness.
- Karate training is not only for the Dojo
- Learning karate is a lifetime journey.
- The beauty in the Way of Karate, it can be applied to everything.
- Karate is like boiling water. If not heated, it will cool down.
- Do not think of winning. Instead, think of not losing.
- Assess and observe your opponent then adjust yourself accordingly
- The outcome of a fight, depends on one's ability to understand weaknesses and strengths
- Think of hands and feet as swords.
- Once you step beyond your own gate, you will face a million enemies.
- Formal stances are for beginners, expert moves naturally.
- Kata can be precise and perfectly performed, real fight is another thing.
- Do not forget the employment of withdrawal of power, the extension or contraction of the body, the swift or leisurely application of technique
- Keep on thinking, and seek new ways

TORA NO MAKI

MY TRADITIONAL KARATE PATHWAY
STRENGTH, SKILL AND KNOWLEDGE

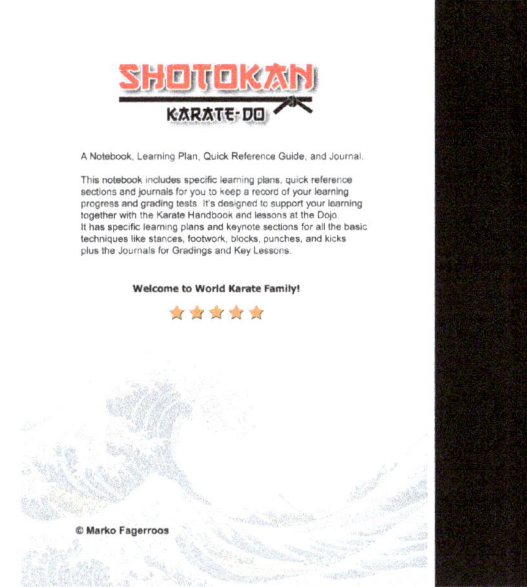
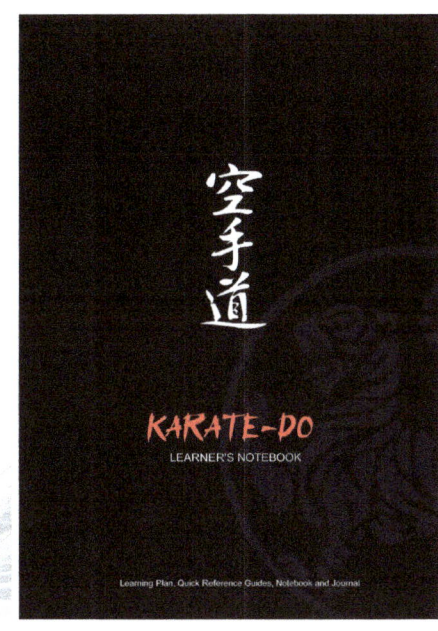

A Notebook, Learning Plan, Quick Reference guide, and Journal.

This new learners' Notebook includes Learning plans, Quick Reference guides and Journals for you to keep a record of your learning progress and grading tests. It's designed to support your learning with the Karate Handbook and the lessons at the Dojo. It has specific Plans and Keynote sections for all the basic Kihon groups like stances, footwork, blocks, punches, and kicks, plus the Journals for Gradings and Key Lessons.

www.ingramcontent.com/pod-product-compliance
Lightning Source LLC
Chambersburg PA
CBHW062040290426
44109CB00026B/2685